W9-APC-755

THE READER'S COMPANION

THE READER'S COMPANION

A Book Lover's Guide to the Most Important Books in Every Field of Knowledge as Chosen by the Experts

Fred Bratman and Scott Lewis

New York

For information address Hyperion,
114 Fifth Avenue, New York, New York 10011.

General Editor: Karen Watts

Library of Congress Cataloging-in-Publication Data

Bratman, Fred.
The reader's companion : a book lover's guide to the most important books in every field of knowledge, as chosen by the experts. Fred Bratman and Scott Lewis.
p. cm.
ISBN 0 - 7868 - 6009 - X
1. Bibliography – United States – Best books. I. Lewis, Scott, 1952- . II. Title .
Z1035. B833 1994
011' .73' 0973 – dc20 93 - 48971
CIP

First Edition

10 9 8 7 6 5 4 3 2 1

Contents

INTRODUCTION

We first came to the idea of *The Reader's Companion* from our own love of books. The search for just the right book on a particular subject has always seemed an hit-or-miss affair, and the effort to match a book with a mood or personal need is usually even more of a crapshoot. Scanning best-seller lists only tells you what everyone else is reading, not necessarily which books are vital to a broad, lifelong experience in enlightenment. It occurred to us that asking a variety of individuals, well-known in their fields, what books they'd recommend might give interested readers a great place to begin that exercise.

Consequently, we asked a wide range of people for book selections in their fields of expertise, or for the books that have significantly affected their lives or careers. We approached scholars, artists, scientists, politicians, novelists, and business leaders. The responses we received were thoughtful, compelling, and entirely inspiring. Some contributors crafted essays, weaving together a selection of books with personal explanations of their choices. Others sent unadorned lists, which were no less inspiring or revealing for their simplicity. Occasionally, contributors noted titles of books that have had a lasting personal influence on them. And in certain subject areas, such as journalism or fiction, we found that they did not read about their field, they just did it, and instead highlighted works that have affected their lives and thinking.

The result is the wonderful mosaic that is *The Reader's Companion*. This book is not comprehensive in that it does not purport to feature the experts' advice in every category imaginable. The subject areas covered tend to be broad — there are books on food, but not wine; science, but not chemistry; the environment, not rainforests. And the luck of the draw played its part in the book's makeup as well, for in some subject areas we hoped to cover in depth, we did not receive the number of responses we anticipated. But the overall pattern is rich and compelling, more so even than we imagined possible at the outset.

It is our hope that *The Reader's Companion* will spur the general reader to dip or delve into subjects that are popular and academic, broad and specialized, contemporary and classic. This treasure trove of inspiration would not of course have been possible without the cooperation of the esteemed contributors. We are deeply appreciative of their generosity and thoughtfulness — and their commitment, with us, to working with the Literacy Volunteers of America to encourage reading. A portion of the proceeds from the sale of *The Reader's Companion* will go to support that organization.

We would also like to acknowledge several people who helped see our idea reach fruition. Our agent, Loretta Fidel, encouraged us during periods of doubt and indecision; Karen Watts of Cloverdale Press and Mary Ann Naples of Hyperion kept our eyes on the finish line and the final product; and Robert Miller of Hyperion, who liked our idea from the start and whose enthusiasm never flagged. And finally, our greatest sources of inspiration, our wives, Robin Gail Steinberg and Alice Swenson.

Fred Bratman and Scott Lewis

CHAPTER 1
CURRENT AFFAIRS

The term "current affairs" couldn't have a more literal meaning than it does now, in the instant information age. The actions of governments or individuals in power reverberate across the globe in the most immediate ways. Images of international importance are broadcast live worldwide, so, for instance, anyone practically anywhere was able to observe the war in the Persian Gulf as if tuning in to the World Series. What's current is so current, evolving within view of the world on a minute-by-minute basis, that one public issue dissolves into the next long before the last has come close to being explored or resolved. All of which makes one of the most popular choices of contributors throughout this book so interesting: Alexis de Tocqueville's *Democracy in America*, first published in 1838, is cited again and again as a title which continues to shed light on contemporary affairs.

DOUG BANDOW ON POLITICS

What is so often lacking in American politics is a sense of history. Thus, Paul Johnson's **Modern Times: The World from the Twenties to the Eighties** should be on any reading list. This book provides an incisive and readable portrait of world events since World War I, a cataclysmic tableau that should be understood by everyone as we prepare to move into the next century.

In fact, it is useful to back up a bit, starting with the sad story of how the world slid into the conflagration that set the tone for the rest of the century. In **The German Wars: 1914-1945**, D.J. Goodspeed finds responsibility for the conflict to be much more evenly spread than commonly thought; his analysis is compelling and provocative, a wonderful tonic to the bland conventional wisdom peddled in most schools.

How the U.S. moved from republic to empire and got entangled in Europe's senseless bloodletting is explored by Walter Karp's brilliant **The Politics of War**. Karp's analysis has particular relevance today as Washington seeks to adjust its foreign policy to the post–Cold War era.

Indeed, that promiscuous reliance on military force in conflicts of little security importance to America is not worth the human cost should be obvious from perusing Paul Fussell's **Wartime: Understanding and Behavior in the Second World War**, a powerful depiction of what really happens in war. Those determined to avoid the sort of mistakes that have led to this century's global slugfests should also pick up John Mueller's **Retreat from Doomsday: The Obsolescence of Major War**, a sophisticated look at this century's march toward and, hopefully, away from global conflict.

Directed more at the home front is Charles Murray's **In Pursuit: Of Happiness and Good Government**, a delightful discussion of the proper role of the state in human affairs. Murray avoids ideological cant while making a compelling case that the only appropriate use of the state is to promote people's "pursuit of happiness," the wonderful phrase reaching back to America's Declaration of Independence and beyond.

Why the federal government long abandoned such a role is evident from two very different books. Robert Higg's **Crisis and Leviathan: Critical Episodes in the Growth of American Government** reviews how economic calamity and military conflict repeatedly and irrevocably expanded state power and diminished individual liberty. David Stockman's **The Triumph of Politics: Why the Reagan Revolution Failed** provides an entertaining — and only slightly self-serving — account as to how even an alleged radical conservative like Ronald Reagan could preside over the steady expansion of the very government he had long crticized.

The consequences of a free people constantly turning larger areas of their lives over to the control of the political process should be evident enough from the collapse of Communism, if not the severe problems in America's own welfare state. But it is useful to review two classics from liberals in the classic tradition. One is Friedrich Hayek's **The Road to Serfdom**, which fired an early warning shot on the inherent and inevitable flaws of collectivism. The second is Milton Friedman's **Capitalism & Freedom**, in which the distinguished economist unashamedly endorsed both economic and personal liberty at a time when few questioned the beneficence of the government.

Still, the political dream lives. How can otherwise reasonable people have such wildly different views as to proper policy? Providing the answer is Thomas Sowell's **A Conflict of Visions: Ideological Origins of Political Struggles**. Perhaps more than any other book, *A Conflict of Visions* explains the basis for the bitter, even violent ideological fault-lines in American politics today. Alao useful in this regard is James Davison Hunter's **Culture Wars: The Struggle to Define America**. Hunter's exploration of the increasingly divisive role of religion in American public life should help all sides better understand — even respect — their opponents.

Such an accommodation is important because we eschew a debate over values at our own peril. In **The Naked Public Square: Religion and**

Democracy in America, Richard John Neuhaus makes an eloquent plea for the legitimacy of religious values in public discourse. The alternative, he warns, is "the naked public square," a public arena shorn of religion — with the sort of horrendous consequences evident to anyone who reads *Modern Times*. And obviously that is in no one's interest.

DOUG BANDOW is a Senior Fellow at the Cato Institute. He is the author and editor of several books, including *The Politics of Plunder: Misgovernment in Washington* and *Beyond Good Intentions: A Biblical View of Politics*.

HEATHER BOOTH ON ACTIVISM

Organize! A Manual for Activists in the 1990s by Kim Bobo, Jackie Kendall, and Steve Max of the Midwest Academy. The best description of tactics, strategic planning, and context.

Rules for Radicals and **Reveille for Radicals**, both by Saul Alinsky. The classics with a community perspective.

The Grassroots Fundraising Book by Joan Flanagan. Techniques and examples.

Parting the Waters by Taylor Branch. For the history of the early civil rights movement and deep insight into the traits of leadership, organization, and moral vision that are required to make activism a life commitment.

Backlash by Susan Faludi. A perspective on women's role in society and some of the concerns that demand our attention.

People's History of the U.S. and **The Twentieth Century, A People's History** by Howard Zinn. To remind us how people make history and how we can take the future into our own hands.

The Politics of Rich and Poor by Kevin Phillips. The economic divisions and politics which brought us to this point.

Who Will Tell the People?, by William Greide. An overview of the obstacles and opportunities to building real democracy in the 1990s.

HEATHER BOOTH is field director of the Democratic National Committee and coordinator of the National Health Care Campaign. She is president and founder of the Midwest Academy, a training center for community organizers. She was co-founder and former president of Citizen Action, the largest progressive political organization in the United States. She is co-author, with Harry Boyte and Steve Max, of *Citizen Action and the New American Populism.*

In our time, political speech and writing are
largely the defense of the indefensible.
— George Orwell

BILL BRADLEY ON POLITICS

The following is a list of a few books that have shaped my thinking about the people, the events, and the ideas that make up the political process in America.

The American Political Tradition by Richard Hofstadter.
The Papers of Woodrow Wilson, edited by Arthur Link.
The History of the United States, 1801-1809 by Henry Adams.
The Liberal Tradition in America by Louis Hartz.

BILL BRADLEY has served in the U.S. Senate as a Democrat from New Jersey since 1979. He is the author of *Life on the Run*, a memoir of his pro basketball career.

DAVID BRODER ON POLITICS

All the King's Men by Robert Penn Warren. The classic American political novel, full of insights about the universal motivations of politicians and reporters.

Presidential Power by Richard Neustadt and **The Twilight of the Presidency** by George Reedy. Neustadt writes with great shrewdness about how a President may succeed, and Reedy with even greater wisdom about why so many Presidents fail.

Member of the House: Letters of a Congressman by Clem Miller. The author, who served in the House in the 1960s, gives a wonderfully candid insider's account of life in the legislative branch.

Democracy in America by Alexis de Tocqueville. No one has written about the American character with greater understanding than this 19th century French visitor.

Miracle at Philadelphia by Catherine Drinker Bowen and **The Federalist Papers** by James Madison, Alexander Hamilton, and John Jay. An account of the drama of the framing of the Constitution and the classic exposition of its principles — this is where it all began.

DAVID BRODER is a syndicated political columnist with *The Washington Post*. He has received the Pulitzer Prize for commentary and his books include *The Party's Over*, *Changing of the Guard*, and *Behind the Front Page*.

Democracy is the worst form of government except all those other forms that have been tried from time to time.
— Winston Churchill

RICHARD BROOKHISER ON POLITICS

C. S. Lewis's **The Abolition of Man** describes the cultural context in which modern politics occurs. Friedrich Hayek's **Road to Serfdom** is the classic statement of the inevitable difficulties of economic planning.

The Federalist Papers, by Madison, Hamilton, and Jay, is the owner's manual for the Federal government when it rolled off the assembly line. Harry Jaffa's **Crisis of the House Divided** explains why the machine broke down, and what Abraham Lincoln did about it.

Despite the great number of campaign books, few are good. The best is William F. Buckley, Jr.'s **The Un-Making of a Mayor,** which edges out A. J. Liebling's **The Earl of Louisiana** because Buckley writes as a candidate.

Finally, read Yeats's last poem, **Politics**.

RICHARD BROOKHISER is a senior editor of *National Review* magazine and a columnist for *The New York Observer*. He is the author of *The Outside Story: How Democrats and Republicans Re-Elected Reagan* and *The Way of the WASP.*

JOSEPH CALIFANO ON GOVERNMENT

Democracy in America by Alexis de Tocqueville.
The Seven Storey Mountain by Thomas Merton.
Eisenhower the General and Eisenhower the President by Steven Ambrose.
The Affluent Society by John Kenneth Galbraith.
Parting the Waters by Taylor Branch.
The Critical Calling by Richard McCormick.
The Social Transformation of American Medicine by Paul Starr.

JOSEPH A. CALIFANO, JR. heads the Center on Addiction and Substance Abuse at Columbia University. He was Assistant to the President for Domestic Affairs under Lyndon Johnson and served as Secretary of Health, Education, and Welfare under President Jimmy Carter. His books include *Governing America: An Insider's Report from the White House and the Cabinet; America's Health Care Revolution: Who Lives? Who Dies? Who Pays?;* and *The Triumph and Tragedy of Lyndon Johnson: The White House Years.*

AMITAI ETZIONI ON GOVERNMENT

Daniel Yankelovich's **Coming to Public Judgment** explains in depth and scope unparalleled the way the American people come to form considered choices as to the directions our democracy is to move.

Robert Bellah's **The Good Society** tells the ways we need to change the social/moral climate by paying more attention to core institutions (such as the family, schools, voluntary associations, and religious ones) to make our society good again.

Mary Ann Glendon's **Rights Talk** is a masterful exposition of the way we got off track by overextending the notion of individual rights and neglecting our social responsibilities.

Jane Mansbridge's **Beyond Self Interest** is the best collection to show us what makes people vote and work, and otherwise motivates people to do what needs doing.

William Galston's **Liberal Purposes: Goods, Virtues, and Diversity in the Liberal State** is a major contribution to the current theory of liberalism.

AMITAI ETZIONI is a professor of sociology at George Washington University. He served in the White House as a senior advisor to President Jimmy Carter. His books include *Capital Corruption; The Moral Dimension;* and *The Spirit of Community: Rights, Responsibilities, and the Communitarian Agenda.*

FRANCES FARENTHOLD ON POLITICS

One Easter weekend while I was still in law school I read Alan Paton's **Cry the Beloved Country**. Earlier I had read Richard Wright's **Native Son** as a class assignment. For me, reading Paton's book was a transforming event. Equally affecting for me was reading **The Autobiography of Malcolm X** — it was given to me by my then 15-year-old son 20 years ago. These books helped me to break through a great deal of Southern denial.

FRANCES T. FARENTHOLD is a lawyer and a former politician. She served in the Texas House of Representatives from 1968 to 1972, was the Democratic candidate for governor of Texas in 1972, and chair of the National Women's Political Caucus from 1973 to 1975.

J. WILLIAM FULBRIGHT ON AMERICAN GOVERNMENT

Some of my favorite authors and their work include Alexis de Tocqueville's **Democracy in America**; George Reedy's **Twilight of the Presidency**; James McGregor Burns's **Presidential Government**; Ronald Steele's **Pax Americana**; and a number of works by **Walter Lippmann**, **Barbara Tuchman**, and **David Halberstam**.

J. WILLIAM FULBRIGHT served as United States Senator from Arkansas from 1944 to 1975, and as chairman of the Senate Foreign Relations Committee from 1959 to 1974. His books include *The Arrogance of Power; The Crippled Giant, Old Myths and New Realities;* and *The Price of Empire* (with Seth Tillman).

MARK O. HATFIELD ON GOVERNMENT AND POLITICS

The American Commonwealth by Viscount James Bryce (3 volumes). Lord Bryce, a frequent visitor to the United States and British Ambassador from 1907 to 1913, provides a comprehensive and sympathetic examination of state governments, the Constitution, and the three branches of the Federal government, including their characteristics, functions, and inter-branch relationships. *The American Commonwealth* is generally regarded as one of the classic expositions of politics and government in the United States.

Our Country: The Shaping of America from Roosevelt to Reagan by Michael Barone. A political history of the United States over the past six decades. The author documents political events and trends and also examines social, cultural, economic, and demographic developments over the period.

Corwin and Peltason's Understanding the Constitution by Edward Samuel Corwin and J.W. Peltason, 10th edition. An overview of the background and provisions of the U.S. Constitution, including a clause-by-clause interpretation in both historical and contemporary contexts.

Congress and Its Members by Roger H. Davidson and Walter J. Oleszek, 3rd edition. The structure and functions of the contemporary Congress are examined, including Congress's diverse roles as a representative of the citizens, a working legislature, and a policymaking body.

The Federalist by Alexander Hamilton, James Madison, and John Jay (Harvard University Press edition, Benjamin Fletcher, editor). Three of the founding fathers explain and defend the Constitution. A primary work of great importance which generated widespread public support for the

Constitution when published. This 1961 edition is recommended because of its comprehensive introductory commentary.

The Chief Executive by Louis William Koenig. A study of the presidency, including the origins and development of the office, nomination, and election, and the diverse leadership roles of the President. Also addresses presidential response to various challenges and provides comparisons with other executives, such as mayors, governors, and foreign leaders.

The Party's Just Begun: Shaping Political Parties for America's Future by Larry J. Sabato. The author traces the evolution, structure, and functions of American political parties, with particular emphasis on current developments and projections for the future.

American Political Thought by Max J. Skidmore. A comprehensive overview of the evolution of American political thought, including contending philosophies and trends, from colonial times to the present.

The Power Game: How Washington Works by Hedrick Smith. A journalist's account of the dynamics of the contemporary political process in Washington and the nation. Examines the roles of Congress, the President, the Federal bureaucracy, political parties, and special interest groups in the struggle for public policy formation.

Democracy in America by Alexis de Tocqueville. This work is the result of the author's extended tour of the United States in 1831-32. It examines both the political and social institutions of the United States during the earlier stages of our national development. This book has long been regarded as a classic for its insight into the American democratic experiment.

And consider this political fiction:

Democracy: An American Novel by Henry Adams, first published in 1880. A wealthy New York widow experiences corruption in politics in

Gilded Age Washington. A distinguished American man of letters, the author was the grandson and great-grandson of U.S. Presidents. Perhaps the prototypical political novel.

Advise and Consent by Allen Drury. First published in 1959. Politics and scandal figure in the struggle to confirm a controversial nominee for Secretary of State in mid-20th century America.

All the King's Men by Robert Penn Warren, first published in 1946. Traces the rise and fall of Willy Stark, the fictional populist demagogue governor of a Southern state in the 1930s.

MARK O. HATFIELD has served in the U.S. Senate as a Republican from Oregon since 1966 and was formerly governor of Oregon from 1958 to 1966. His books include *Conflict and Conscience*; *Between a Rock and a Hard Place;* and *Confessing Christ and Doing Politics.*

ELLIOT RICHARDSON ON LEADERSHIP

One book stands out as important to the understanding of leadership: **The Killer Angels** by Michael Shaara. The story of the Battle of Gettysburg from the perspective of its principal actors, it depicts a wide range of attributes and styles of leadership with remarkable sensitivity and imagination.

Joshua Lawrence Chamberlain of the 20th Maine comes through as the most gifted leader I have ever read about anywhere, and since reading *The Killer Angels* I've learned enough about Chamberlain to be confident that Shaara's portrait of him is accurate.

ELLIOT L. RICHARDSON is a senior partner with the law firm of Milbank Tweed Hadley & McCloy. His numerous former government posts include Secretary of Health, Education, and Welfare, and Attorney General, under President Nixon, and Ambassador to Great Britain and Secretary of Commerce under President Ford.

JEFFREY RICHELSON ON INTELLIGENCE AND NATIONAL SECURITY

Her Majesty's Secret Service by Christopher Andrew. An account of the development of the British intelligence services, from Elizabethan England to the end of World War II.

The Puzzle Palace: A Report of NSA, America's Most Secret Agency by James Bamford. The development and operations of the U.S. National Security Agency, responsible for the collection of signals intelligence.

Deep Black: Space Espionage and National Security by William E. Burrows. A fascinating examination of America's aerial and space reconnaissance systems.

Hitler's Spies: German Military Intelligence in World War II by David Kahn. An in-depth examination, based on captured German documents, of the Nazi empire's elaborate espionage network. Because of the definitive end of the Nazi regime and the availability of its most secret archives, this may be the best documented book on intelligence.

The Cheka: Lenin's Political Police by George Leggett. A detailed account of the first modern totalitarian secret police organization — the forerunner of the KGB.

The CIA and the Cult of Intelligence by Victor Marchetti and John Marks. The view from the inside by a former CIA official.

Wilderness of Mirrors by David Martin. CIA counterintelligence operations and the career of James Jesus Angleton.

Armour Against Fate: British Military Intelligence in the First World War by Michael Occleshaw. Relying on primary documents, the author has produced a detailed picture of the full range of British intelligence activities in the Great War.

The Man Who Kept the Secrets: Richard Helms and the CIA by Thomas Powers. An extremely well-written and fascinating study of career intelligence officer and former CIA chief Richard Helms. The extensive footnotes are a bonus in themselves, worth the price of the book.

The Soviet Estimate: U.S. Intelligence and Russian Military Strength by John Prados. A scholarly and readable account of how well the U.S. intelligence community estimated the capabilities of the Soviet military.

OSS: The Secret History of America's First Central Intelligence Agency by R. Harris Smith. A look at the diverse activities of America's first centralized intelligence organization, which operated during World War II.

The Spymasters of Israel by Stewart Steven. The best, albeit not the most recent, of the multitude of books on Israeli intelligence.

JEFFREY T. RICHELSON is an intelligence expert and author. His books include *America's Secret Eyes in Space*; *The U.S. Intelligence Community*; *American Espionage and the Soviet Target*; and *A Century of Spies: Intelligence in the Twentieth Century.*

JOSEPH SISCO ON DIPLOMACY

Politics Among Nations by Hans Morgenthau. This book is still the best on explaining the fundamental nature of international relations.

Gorbachev's Russia and American Foreign Policy, edited by Seweryn Bialer and Michael Mandelbaum. A comprehensive analysis in a series of articles combining historical perspective and current developments.

Great Decisions published by the Foreign Policy Association. An annual evaluation of the more important foreign policy issues. Excellent for succinct evaluation and for use in a classroom setting.

White House Years and **Years of Upheaval** by Henry Kissinger. In two volumes, a thorough synthesis of the strategy and tactics of diplomacy.

JOSEPH SISCO was a leading career foreign service officer, serving as Assistant Secretary of State for Near East-South Asia from 1969 to 1974, and Undersecretary of State for Political Affairs from 1974 to 1976. He was president of American University from 1976 to 1980.

OLIVER STONE ON POLITICS

Buckminster Fuller's **Critical Path**. A world view of economics going back to Phoenician times and how economics ultimately controls politics and government.

L. Fletcher Prouty's **JFK: The CIA, Vietnam, and the Plot to Assassinate John F. Kennedy**. Opens up the horror of modern American history with reasons behind the paramilitary coup d'état in Dallas in November 1963.

Paul Johnson's **Modern Times**. A cold analysis of how sentimentality and fashion have distorted history and justice. Also an analysis of perception and how we view history.

Howard Zinn's **A People's History of the United States**. The antithesis to Johnson's book — in many ways, opens the eyes to the fate of the common man in American history.

William Blum's **The CIA: A Forgotten History**. A shocker, dispassionate and totally grounded in fact, it is an undiscovered masterpiece.

OLIVER STONE is a screenwriter, director, and producer. His screenplays include "Midnight Express" and "Salvador." Movies that he wrote and directed include "Platoon," "Wall Street," and "JFK."

ANTHONY BOUZA ON LAW ENFORCEMENT

These books are written by some of the most eminent scholars and thinkers in the field and offer broad and deep insights into the real and complex issues facing law enforcement in America.

Violence and the Police by William H. Westley.
Varieties of Police Behavior by James Q. Wilson.
Police Leadership in America: Crisis and Opportunity by William Geller.
Policing a Free Society by Herman Goldstein.
Criminal Careers and Career Criminals by Alfred Blumstein et al.
The Challenge of Crime in a Free Society: A Report by the President's Commission on Law Enforcement and the Administration of Justice, U.S. Government Printing Office.
The Police and the Public by Albert J. Reiss, Jr.

ANTHONY V. BOUZA was a New York City policeman for nearly 25 years, reaching the rank of Borough Commander before serving as Chief of Police of Minneapolis from 1980 to 1988. He is the author of *The Police Mystique: An Insider's Look at Cops, Crime and the Criminal Justice System,* and *How to Stop Crime.*

EDNA BUCHANAN ON CRIME

The Complete Works of Shakespeare. For every foible, folly, and passion unique to mankind. I met Othello, Romeo and Juliet, King Lear, and Hamlet regularly on the streets of Miami. Some bad days on the police beat I met them all.

The Complete Tales and Poems of Edgar Allan Poe. For the melancholy beauty and sheer terror of the dark side.

The Annotated Sherlock Holmes: The Four Novels and the Fifty-six Short Stories by Sir Arthur Conan Doyle. For the logic.

Raintree County by Ross Lockridge, Jr. For the poetry of America's violent history, and the star-crossed lovers.

The Alexandria Quartet: Justine, **Balthazar**, **Mountolive**, and **Clea** by Lawrence Durrell. For the pulse and heartbeat of a teeming, sweltering, and mysterious city and its inhabitants.

The Garden Party by Katherine Mansfield. For the delicacy of small moments.

EDNA BUCHANAN writes books. Her novels include *Contents Under Pressure* and *Nobody Lives Forever*. Her nonfiction books include *The Corpse Had a Familiar Face* and *Never Let Them See You Cry*. She won the Pulitzer Prize for journalism in 1986, for general reporting for her work on the police beat for *The Miami Herald*.

NORMAN DORSEN ON THE CONSTITUTION

We the People: Foundations by Bruce Ackerman.
The Least Dangerous Branch by Alexander Bickel.
The Burger Court: The Counter-Revolution that Wasn't, edited by Vincent Blasi.
The Bill of Rights by Irving Brandt.
Free Speech in the United States by Zechariah Chafee, Jr.

The Role of the Supreme Court in American Government by Archibald Cox.
Taking Rights Seriously by Ronald Dworkin.
The System of Freedom of Expression by Thomas I. Emerson.
Roe v. Wade by Marian Faux.
Speech and Law in a Free Society by Franklyn Haiman.
The Spirit of Liberty by Learned Hand, 3rd edition.
Simple Justice by Richard Kluger.
The National Security Constitution by Harold Koh.
Freedom in the Western World from the Dark Ages to the Rise of Democracy by Herbert J. Muller.
The Bill of Rights: A Documentary History by Bernard Schwartz.
American Constitutional Law by Laurence H. Tribe, 2nd edition.
Constitutional Choices by Laurence H. Tribe.

The Creation of the American Republic by Gordon Wood.

NORMAN DORSEN is the Stokes Professor of Law at New York University. After graduation from Harvard University's School of Law, he clerked for U.S. Supreme Court Justice John Marshall Harlan. Dorsen is the author of several books, including *Our Endangered Rights* and *The Evolving Constitution.*

RONALD GOLDSTOCK ON ORGANIZED CRIME

Under the headings "sociological" and "historical," here are works which, (a) at the time they were written, represented the foremost state of knowledge and analysis in existence, (b) have remained classics in the field, and (c) when read in sequence, provide excellent insights into the nature of organized crime.

Under the heading "general" are three important works which are supported and printed by the Government, as well as a modern text which covers recent developments.

Sociological:

The Gang by Frederick M. Thrasher.
Organized Crime in Chicago by John Landesco.
Street Corner Society by William Foote Whyte.
Theft of the Nation by Donald R. Cressey.

Historical:

Brotherhood of Evil by Frederic Sondern, Jr.
Murder, Inc. by Burton Turkus and Sid Feder.
The Valachi Papers by Peter Maas.
The Business of Crime by Humbert S. Nelli.

General:

Task Force Report: Organized Crime (including Appendices), The President's Commission on Law Enforcement and the Administration of Justice.
Rackets Bureaus: The Investigation and Prosecution of Organized Crime (LEAA Prescriptive Package), U.S. Government Printing Office.
Major Issues in Organized Crime Control, National Institute of Justice, Symposium Proceedings, U.S. Government Printing Office.
Organized Crime by Howard Abadinsky.

RONALD GOLDSTOCK is the director of the New York State Organized Crime Task Force. After graduating from Harvard Law School, he joined the Manhattan district attorney's office, heading the rackets bureau. He also teaches at Cornell Law School.

There is one universal law....That law is justice.
Justice forms the cornerstone of each nation's law.
— Alexis de Tocqueville, *Democracy in America*

WILLIAM KUNSTLER ON LAW

Books which I consider to be important to the understanding of law and our system of justice include:

The Nature of the Judicial Process by Benjamin Cardozo.
The Art of Cross Examination by Francis Wellman.
Clarence Darrow for the Defense by Irving Stone.
The Greening of America by Charles Reich.
A Trial on Trial by Lawrence Dennis and Maximillian St. George.

And a book that has had a great deal of impact on my life has been **Collected Poems** by Dylan Thomas.

WILLIAM KUNSTLER is an attorney who has represented many political activists, among them the Freedom Riders in Mississippi, the Chicago Seven, and American Indian Movement leaders. His books include *Beyond a Reasonable Doubt?: The Original Trial of Caryl Chessman* and *...And Justice for All.*

ARTHUR LIMAN ON LAW

The United States Constitution.
The Federalist Papers by Alexander Hamilton, James Madison, and John Jay.
The Common Law by Oliver Wendell Holmes.
The Nature of the Judicial Process by Benjamin Cardozo.

John Marshall's opinion in **Marbury v. Madison.**
The opinion of the court in **Brown v. Board of Education.**

ARTHUR L. LIMAN is a partner in the law firm of Paul, Weiss, Rifkind, Wharton & Garrison. He served as chief counsel to the U.S. Senate Select Committee on Iran-Contra. He was also president of the New York City Legal Aid Society.

JAMES Q. WILSON ON CRIME

Criminal Violence, Criminal Justice by Charles Silberman. Discusses public policy toward crime from a different point of view than my own *Thinking About Crime.*
No Escape by John J. DiIulio. Analyzes the role of prisons in American criminal justice.
Drugs and Crime, edited by Michael Tonry and James Q. Wilson. Essays on the drug problem and its relationship to crime.

JAMES Q. WILSON is a professor of management at the University of California at Los Angeles. He is the author of *Thinking About Crime* and, with Richard J. Herrnstein, *Crime and Human Nature.*

ROBERT MacNEIL

Since I never studied journalism, I am ignorant of textbooks or books that instruct journalists. But I have always been fascinated by the memoirs and biographies of great journalists. These are some I have found inspiring and instructive.

Long before I knew I would become a journalist, as a teenager I read Valentine Williams's, **The World of Action**, an account of a British correspondent for Reuters News Agency. Ten years later I found myself at Reuters getting my basic training, so I still have a soft spot for the book.

I admire the late British writer, Arthur Ransome. Before he became famous as a children's author he was a correspondent for the *Manchester Guardian* during the Russian Revolution. Ransome was close to the major players including Lenin and Trotsky and his **Autobiography** is an extraordinary account.

So are the memoirs of Harrison Salisbury, **Journey for Our Times** and **A Time of Change: A Reporter's Tale for Our Time**. Salisbury is one of the greats still among us: tough, independent, and gritty.

Another great journalist was the late I.F. Stone, the maverick lone-wolf who taught all establishment journalists what one focused reporter can do. Andrew Patner's **I.F. Stone: A Portrait** is a lesson in independence.

Theodore White had many claims to greatness, as a foreign correspondent in China, later as the reporter who transformed American political coverage with his **Making of the President** and subsequent books. His memoir, **In Search of History: A Personal Adventure,** should set any young journalist's typewriter fingers itching and his feet twitching to be off to exotic places.

Henry Brandon's **Special Relationships** is a sophisticated account of life as an international journalist by one of the most urbane of the breed.

No book did more to swell the enrollment in journalism schools than **All the President's Men** by Carl Bernstein and Bob Woodward, the *Washington Post* reporters whose persistence caused the Watergate scandal to unravel.

Morley Safer's **Flashback** is a candid, wry second look at Vietnam by the CBS correspondent whose reporting changed public perceptions of the war.

Edward R. Murrow is the icon of broadcast news and there are many good books about him, some electing him to instant sainthood. My favorite is still **Prime Time: The Life of Edward R. Murrow** by his late colleague, Alexander Kendrick.

Two books of journalism criticism are among my favorites: A. J. Liebling's witty and penetrating essays in **The Wayward Pressman** and Michael Arlen's insights into television in **The Camera Age**, each valuable as literature.

ROBERT MACNEIL, co-anchor of the "MacNeil/Lehrer NewsHour" on PBS, previously worked as a correspondent for NBC and the BBC. He is the author of *The People Machine: The Influence of Television on American Politics* and *The Story of English.*

COKIE ROBERTS

I don't know any books on journalism — I do it, don't study it. On politics, though:

Democracy in America, Alexis de Tocqueville
The Federalist Papers, Alexander Hamilton, James Madison, and John Jay
The Emperor's New Clothes, Hans Christian Andersen
Plato's **Dialogues**

COKIE ROBERTS is a correspondent for ABC News and for National Public Radio.

ROGER ROSENBLATT

Mark Twain, **Huckleberry Finn** — for honor.
Boswell's **The Life of Samuel Johnson** — for wisdom.
Joseph Conrad's novels and stories — for valor.
Joyce Cary, **The Horse's Mouth** — for laughter.
Jonathan Swift's **Gulliver's Travels** — for wit.
Sir Arthur Conan Doyle, **Sherlock Holmes** — for fun.
The plays of **J.M. Synge** — for everything.

ROGER ROSENBLATT is a journalist, author, and playwright. He has won the George Polk Award twice, the Peabody, and the Emmy awards. His books include *The Children of War* and *The Man in the Water.*

LIZ TROTTA

Herodotus: **History**
Winston Churchill: **The History of the English-Speaking Peoples** (4 volumes), **The First World War**, and **The History of the Second World War** (6 volumes)
Thomas Macaulay: **History of England**
Karl Marx: **Das Kapital**
Thomas Paine: **The Rights of Man**
Arthur Koestler: **The Lotus and the Robot**
A.J. Liebling: **The Press**
Theodore White: **Fire in the Ashes**
Adam Smith: **Wealth of Nations**
Alexis de Tocqueville: **Democracy in America**
Jean Larteguy: **The Centurions** and **The Praetorians**
Graham Greene: **The Quiet American**

LIZ TROTTA was the first female television news foreign correspondent. Her assignments for NBC and CBS took her to Saigon, London, and Hong Kong. Her work won her three Emmys. She is also the author of *Fighting for Air: In the Trenches with Television News.*

Power is precarious.
— Herodotus, *Histories*

NICHOLAS VON HOFFMAN

I don't know of a good book on journalism, although journalists have written many good books.

On politics, the writings of **John Locke**, **John Stuart Mill**, and **Lord Bryce**. And in the 20th century, for me as an American, **Revolt of the Masses** by Jose Ortega y Gasset and **Brave New World** by Aldous Leonard Huxley have been important.

As for the books I'd take to a desert island, I would take along a trunk full of **Trollope**, **Faulkner**, and, say, John Updike's **Rabbit** series.

NICHOLAS VON HOFFMAN has written for the *Chicago Daily News* and the *Washington Post*, and has reported for "60 Minutes" and CBS radio. He is a columnist for the *New York Observer*, and is the author of many books, including the novel *Organized Crime*, as well as *Citizen Cohn* and *Capitalist Fools*.

CHAPTER 2
THE ARTS

The book lists shared in the area of the arts are predictably wonderful for book lovers. Those who manage to make their way through these lists without being compelled to take a look, perhaps again, at Chekhov's stories or Melville's *Moby Dick* simply cannot be moved. It is clear that our contributors are deeply devoted to and dependent on the works of others, and are grateful for the inspiration their forebears or colleagues have provided. It makes the reader feel, for his or her part, somehow an integral part of the historical life cycle of art and literature.

FREDERICK BARTHELME

Heinrich von Kleist, **The Marquise of O & Other Stories**
Ivan Goncharov, **Oblomov**
James Joyce, **Dubliners**
James M. Cain, **Serenade**
Junichiro Tanizaki, **The Key** and **Seven Japanese Tales**
Yasunari Kawabata, **The Master of Go** and **Beauty and Sadness**

Jean Rhys, **Good Morning, Midnight**; **Quartet**; and **After Leaving Mr. MacKenzie**
Samuel Beckett, **Endgame**
Alain Robbe-Grillet, **For a New Novel: Essays on Fiction**
Roland Barthes, **Writing Degree Zero** and **Elements of Semiology**
William Gass, **Fiction and the Figures of Life**
Philip Stevick, **The Theory of the Novel** (an anthology)
Walker Percy, **The Message in the Bottle**
And the writings of **Dickens**, **Raymond Chandler**, **Marquez**, **Soseki**, **Kafka**, and **Chekhov**.

FREDERICK BARTHELME is a writer and a professor of English at the University of Southern Mississippi. His books include *Moon Deluxe*; *Tracer*; *Two Against One*; and *Complaint*.

LAWRENCE BLOCK

Several books influenced me greatly in that I read and was hugely impressed by them at about the time I was becoming aware of literature and of my own calling thereto. These come readily to mind:

James T. Farrell, **Studs Lonigan**
Thomas Wolfe, **Of Time and the River**
John Steinbeck, **The Grapes of Wrath**
John Dos Passos, **U.S.A.**

When I began to have some acceptance in the field of crime fiction, I read whole libraries of the stuff. Much of what I read had an impact. I'll list some individual titles, but I didn't really read individual books; I gulped down complete works.

Dashiell Hammett, **The Maltese Falcon**
Raymond Chandler, **The Long Goodbye**
Fredric Brown, **The Fabulous Clipjoint**
Agatha Christie, **The Murder of Roger Ackroyd**
Rex Stout, **Black Orchids**

The works of one American novelist and short story writer have had a continuing influence on my writing and, I shouldn't wonder, on my world view. I've read all of his books over and over, and I wouldn't be surprised if I get rather more out of them than he put into them. I'll mention two favorites: John O'Hara, **Ten North Frederick** and **From the Terrace**.

I should mention a very uneven writer who, in his best work, made enormously difficult narrative tasks look effortless and natural: Somerset Maugham, **Cakes and Ale** and **The Moon and Sixpence**.

And a man I wish I'd had a chance to meet, who wrote relatively little and died too soon: Walter Tevis, **The Queen's Gambit** and **The Color of Money**.

LAWRENCE BLOCK is a mystery writer and the creator of Matt Scudder. His many novels include *The Burglar Who Liked to Quote Kipling,* which won the Nero Wolfe award; *Eight Million Ways to Die; When the Sacred Ginmill Closes,* which won the Japanese Maltese Falcon award; and *A Walk Among the Tombstones.*

RAY BRADBURY

The novels of **Jules Verne**.
The novels of **H. G. Wells**.
All of the novels by Edgar Rice Burroughs, including **Tarzan of the Apes, John Carter,** and **Warlord of Mars.**
Buck Rogers, **Flash Gordon**, **Tarzan**, and **Prince Valiant** comic strips, 1939-1960. Pivotal stuff for a 9-year-old and a 16-year-old, and a 25-year-old, all leading up to *The Martian Chronicles* when I was 30 and *Farenheit 451* when I was 33.
All of the plays of **George Bernard Shaw**, plus all of his incredible, bright prefaces.
The poetry of **Alexander Pope**.
Hamlet. Shakespeare.
Moby Dick. Melville, which led up to my writing the screenplay of the book for John Huston.
All the incredible novels of Thomas Love Peacock, including **Headlong Hall** and **Gryll Grange.**
All the stories of **Edgar Allan Poe**.
All the poems of **Emily Dickinson**.
The short stories of **Eudora Welty**.
The stories of **Katherine Anne Porter**.
The stories of **Edith Wharton** and **Jessamyn West**.
All of the plays of **Molière**.
All of the stories of **John Collier**.

RAY BRADBURY writes novels, short stories, poems, plays, and screenplays. His works include *Farenheit 451*; *Something Wicked This Way Comes*;

and *Green Shadows, White Whole*. His short story collections include *The Martian Chronicles* and *The Machineries of Joy*. Bradbury has recently written his first two detective novels.

ROSELLEN BROWN

Fiction writers must read more than fiction, therefore:

Alexis de Tocqueville, **Democracy in America**. Because he understood our contemporary America long before it existed.

Anton Chekhov: The stories. The plays, too. Because he loved even his most unlovable characters without sentimentality.

Emily Dickinson, **Collected Poems**. Because she was absolutely original, alone with her passionate imagination.

Tillie Olsen, **Tell Me a Riddle.** Because she dared deep feeling without much regard for fashion or patience for cynicism.

Henry James, **The Art of the Novel: Critical Prefaces**. Because these are oblique, quirky, challenging speculations about the way novels work.

Art Spiegelman, **Maus I**, and **II**. Because he proves that there is nothing that can't be done, that no forms can be called too frivolous for serious purposes.

ROSELLEN BROWN is a novelist and short story writer. Her novels include *Tender Mercies*, *Civil Wars*, and *Before and After*.

JAMES LEE BURKE

As a fiction writer, I can think of no finer books than these five from which to learn style and the creation of character:

The Sound and the Fury by William Faulkner.
The Collected Short Stories of Ernest Hemingway by Ernest Hemingway.
The Great Gatsby by F. Scott Fitzgerald.
Studs Lonigan by James T. Farrell.
Of Mice and Men by John Steinbeck.

JAMES LEE BURKE is a novelist. Before turning to writing full time he was a surveyor, oil field worker, social worker, newspaper reporter, and college teacher. His novels include *To the Bright and Shining Sun*, *Black Cherry Blues,* and *A Morning for Flamingos.*

I love to sail forbidden seas
and land on barbarous coasts.
— Herman Melville, *Moby Dick*

JOHN CASEY

Literature is not ordered knowledge, as is philosophy or architecture. I can't help but confuse it with life. There are so many books that I love that I've had to limit this list to eight works, each of which happened to be a comfort. They all portray distress and destruction, but their sense of life is enlarging.

Speak, Memory by Vladimir Nabokov.
George Orwell's essays.
À la Recherche du Temps Perdu by Marcel Proust.
Stories by Alice Munro, especially **Oranges and Apples** and **Labor Day Weekend.**
Stories by Anton Chekhov, especially **In the Ravine**, **The Darling**, **Peasants**, and **Lady with the Dog**.
Red Cavalry by Isaac Babel.
Stories by **Rudyard Kipling**.
Moby Dick by Herman Melville.

JOHN CASEY is a novelist and a professor of English at the University of Virginia. His novels include *An American Romance*, *South Country*, and *Spartina*, which won the National Book Award.

DOMINICK DUNNE

The Way We Live Now by Anthony Trollope. I have read his novel many times and learned a great deal about using a huge cast of characters from it, and the subtleties of class differences.

Brideshead Revisited by Evelyn Waugh. A superb depiction of a large family both held together and destroyed by their religion.

War and Peace by Leo Tolstoy. This is to me the greatest historical novel. A vast array of characters, clearly defined, a wonderful delineation of the classes, and the best written war scenes, showing the tragedy and madness of it.

The Great Gatsby by F. Scott Fitzgerald. Such a great use of the narrator, Nick Cartwright.

The Razor's Edge by W. Somerset Maugham. I reread this book every couple of years. I love the idea of Maugham using himself as the narrator.

DOMINICK DUNNE is a novelist and a former television and movie producer and writer. Movies he produced include "The Boys in the Band" and "Panic in Needle Park." His novels include *The Two Mrs. Grenvilles, People Like Us, An Inconvenient Woman*, and *A Season in Purgatory.*

MARILYN FRENCH

The authors who triggered my thought most when I was young were Nietzsche, especially **Beyond Good and Evil**, and Dostoyevsky, especially **The Brothers Karamazov**.

As a young adult trapped in the life and thinking of the 1950s, I was most illuminated by Simone de Beauvoir's **The Second Sex**, Doris Lessing's **The Golden Notebook**, and Christina Stead's **The Man Who Loved Children**.

The books that have been most important in expanding my intellectual or emotional horizons in recent years are two novels—Toni Morrison's **Beloved** and Sembene Ousmane's **God's Bits of Wood**—and an anthropological study of the poor in northeast Brazil, Nancy Scheper-Hughes's **Death Without Weeping**.

MARILYN FRENCH is a novelist, essayist, and literary scholar. Her works of non-fiction include Shakespeare's *Division of Experience*; *Beyond Power: On Women, Men and Morals*; and *The War Against Women*. Her novels include *The Women's Room* and *Her Mother's Daughter*.

❧

Whatever is done from love always
occurs beyond good and evil.
— Friedrich Nietzsche, *Beyond Good and Evil*

❧

GAIL GODWIN

Emma by Jane Austen.
Middlemarch by George Eliot.
The Portrait of a Lady by Henry James.
Jane Eyre by Charlotte Brontë.
St. Mawr by D. H. Lawrence.
The Golden Notebook by Doris Lessing.

GAIL GODWIN is a novelist and short-story writer. Her novels include *The Odd Woman, A Mother and Two Daughters,* and *Father Melancholy's Daughter.*

OSCAR HIJUELOS

For American literature, whose finest works seem to lean towards first person narrative, I suggest the following:

Adventures of Huckleberry Finn by Mark Twain.
Catcher in the Rye by J.D. Salinger.
Stop-Time by Frank Conroy.
Come Back, Dr. Caligari by Donald Barthelme.
Edisto by Padgett Powell.
Bright Lights, Big City by Jay McInerney.

These books seem to follow a tradition of "pure voice" — the link between Huck Finn, Catcher, and Edisto seems especially strong — as if the two latter writers were much influenced — it's my guess — by Mr. Twain. In any case, I think you would find these books a good introduction to a feisty, fairly fine-tuned, literary sensibility. Also, for my money, anything by **Willa Cather** and **Carson McCullers**.

A second category of American literature, naturalism, would include the works of **Frank Norris**, **Stephen Crane**, **Hemingway**, and **Advertisements for Myself** by Norman Mailer.

I would also suggest an "international" category (for the more adventurously inclined):

Anything by **Jorge Luis Borges**.
Pedro Paramo by Juan Rulfo.
One Hundred Years of Solitude by Gabriel García Márquez.
The works of **Italo Calvino**.
The Third Policeman by Flann O'Brien.
The Tree by Maria Luisa Bombal.
The Tin Drum by Günter Grass.
Union Street by Pat Barker.
Memoirs of Hadrian by Marguerite Yourcenar.

OSCAR HIJUELOS is a novelist. His books include *Our House in the Last World, Mambo Kings Play Songs of Love,* and *The Fourteen Sisters of Emilio Montez O'Brien.*

ROBERT LUDLUM

Shakespeare. At least 20 of his 36 plays of the Folios, especially the histories based on the chronicles of Holinshed and Froissart. Why else? The language! It's never been equaled.

All the King's Men by Robert Penn Warren. A magnificent character study of a messianic politician in the gamey environs of American politics at its uniquely most corrupt. Wonderful narrative and sharp, penetrating dialogue.

Marvels of the Orient by Richard Halliburton. One of the explorer's most colorful books detailing his travels in the Far East. Halliburton was not merely an adventurer (sailor, pilot, mountain climber, etc.) but also a writer who captured the exotic essence of wherever he traveled in words.

All of the above, in one way or another, have helped me grasp the tools of fiction as I have come to understand them. As disparate as they may appear, each is unique in style, breadth, narrative, dialogue, humor, and description.

ROBERT LUDLUM is a novelist and a former actor and theatrical producer. His popular thrillers include *The Rhinemann Exchange, The Bourne Identity, The Icarus Agenda,* and *The Scorpio Illusion.*

MICHAEL MALONE

Laurence Sterne, **Tristram Shandy**
Henry Fielding, **Tom Jones**
Charles Dickens, **David Copperfield**
William Thackeray, **Vanity Fair**
George Eliot, **Middlemarch**
Leo Tolstoy, **War and Peace**
Robert Louis Stevenson, **Treasure Island**
Mark Twain, **Huckleberry Finn**
F. Scott Fitzgerald, **The Great Gatsby**
William Faulkner, **The Hamlet**

These 10 novels had, I think, the most intense and immediate impact on me as novels, as worlds of fiction so large and so realized that they swept over and blotted out the so-called "real world." My sense of the architecture of the novel comes from my early reading of these books.

MICHAEL MALONE is a writer and a college instructor. His novels include *Dingley Falls, Uncivil Seasons,* and *The Passionate Pilgrim.*

IRIS MURDOCH

The Bible.
The complete works of **William Shakespeare.**
War and Peace by Tolstoy.
The Brothers Karamazov by Dostoyevsky.

Our Mutual Friend by Dickens.
À la Recherche du Temps Perdu by Proust (in French).
Wolf Solent by John Cowper Powys.
The poetic works of **Pushkin** (in Russian with English translation).
The poetic works of **Paul Celan** (in German with English translation).
La Divina Commedia by Dante (in Italian with English translation).

IRIS MURDOCH is a novelist, playwright, and former lecturer in philosophy at Oxford University. Her works of nonfiction include *Sartre: Romantic Rationalist* and *The Fire and the Sun: Why Plato Banned the Artists.* Her novels include *The Flight from the Enchanter*; *The Sea, the Sea*, which won the Booker prize; *The Philosopher's Pupil*; and *The Good Apprentice.*

Pure and complete sorrow is
as impossible as pure and complete joy.
— Leo Tolstoy, *War and Peace*

GLORIA NAYLOR

I can chart the making of my career as a writer from the books that have influenced me from childhood to a very late "coming of age" at 30 when I finally found my voice. They are in somewhat of a chronological order:

Grimm's Fairy Tales, which taught me that there are no limits to the magic that can happen in one's life.

Jane Eyre by Charlotte Brontë was given to me by my seventh grade teacher, because she believed that it was the book every young girl should read before her 14th birthday. It also helped to shape my conviction that a novel should, first and foremost, tell a good story.

The Bible, which gave me a guide for forming the principles to live a reasonable life free from harm to myself or others; as well as unending drama on both the cosmic and personal scale. And the language, the heart-stopping language.

Native Son by Richard Wright came to me when I was seeking an understanding of what it meant to be black in America. It was the first book I read as an adult that made me cry.

Memoirs of a Dutiful Daughter by Simone de Beauvoir allowed me to claim meaning to those precious moments in my girlhood as a girlhood. Being a woman is different; and not only is that all right, it should be celebrated.

The Bluest Eye by Toni Morrison was the river into which all those other tributaries emptied. The language. The magic. The specificity of my experiences as a black female. A voice calling for others to join the chorus. I did.

GLORIA NAYLOR is a novelist. Her books include *The Women of Brewster Place*, which received the National Book Award, *Linden Hills,* and *Bailey's Cafe.*

JOYCE CAROL OATES

Essential to an understanding of ongoing American fiction are the yearly volumes **Prize Stories: The O'Henry Awards** and **The Best American Short Stories**. Since 1989, **The Pushcart Prize: The Best of the Small Presses**, edited by Bill Henderson, has become a staple of literary publishing and is essential reading for young writers.

Essential to an understanding of American literary culture — its diversity and what might be called its spiritual individualism — are such works of beauty and mystery as **Emily Dickinson**'s poetry, Whitman's **Leaves of Grass**, Melville's **Moby Dick**, Hawthorne's **The Scarlet Letter** and short stories, the tales of **Poe**, and, not least, the writings of **Henry David Thoreau**. But this is just a beginning.

JOYCE CAROL OATES is a novelist, short story writer, poet, and critic. Her novels include *them*, which received the National Book Award; *Bellefleur; Bloodsmoor Romance*; *Black Water: A Novel*; and *Foxfire: Confessions of a Girl Gang.*

CYNTHIA OZICK

As you can see, my reading life remains mainly closeted in the 19th century. Reading is also (and often essentially) rereading; this applies not only to individuals, but to centuries, too. Some centuries reread previous centuries (as the Renaissance reread the Greeks). And though Graetz, for instance, has been superseded by many contemporary historians (the great Salo Barron among them), I continue to feel gratitude for the historical vision he aroused in me. And I will go on and on cherishing the writers that inflamed my youth — which is probably why the list I submit to you today would have been the list I might have submitted at age 25.

Leo Baeck, **Judaism and Christianity** (especially one essay therein, **Romantic Religion**)
Heinrich Graetz, **History of the Jews**
Milton Himmelfarb, **The Jews of Modernity**
Leon Edel, **Henry James: A Life**
Anton Chekhov, all the short stories, especially **Ward No. Six**
E. M. Forster, all the novels, stories, and essays
George Eliot, **Middlemarch** and **Daniel Deronda**
Jane Austen, all her novels, especially **Emma** and **Persuasion**
Leo Tolstoy, **Anna Karenina**
Joseph Conrad, **Youth** and **Heart of Darkness**

CYNTHIA OZICK is a novelist, short story writer, and critic. Her books include *Trust; Levitation: Five Fictions;* and *The Messiah of Stockholm.*

ROBERT B. PARKER

Certainly Raymond Chandler's books influenced me, especially the earlier ones: **The Big Sleep**, **Farewell My Lovely**, **Lady in the Lake**, **The High Window**.

I was also influenced by Scott Fitzgerald's **Great Gatsby**, all of

Hemingway (particularly the short stories), all of Faulkner (particularly the long version of **The Bear**). I have a Ph.D. in English, which leads one to read (if not always understand) most things since Caxton, and it is not easy to sort out influences. It is somehow ludicrous to cite **Shakespeare**.

There were also the novels of **Joseph Altschuler**, **Batman** comics, **Al Capp**, *Black Mask Magazine*, **Uncle Remus**, and **Winnie the Pooh** (read to me by my father), **The Maltese Falcon**, the poetry of Eliot and Frost, Henry James's **The Ambassadors**, a short story called **Livvie** by Eudora Welty. That's probably enough.

ROBERT B. PARKER writes mystery novels and is the creator of the private investigator Spencer. Since 1974, Parker has written at least one Spencer novel a year. Before turning to fiction, Parker was a professor of English at Northeastern University.

MARGE PIERCY

Scriptures and **Midrash**. I can't separate the importance of the two. The first is rich and sparse at once; the second shows you how any tale has a hundred interpretations and as many points of view as there are people who can tell it.

Ulysses, James Joyce. I read it six times through and once aloud before I was 22 and it taught me an enormous amount about language, myth, and the imagination.

Moby Dick, Herman Melville. Another book I reread and read aloud. He caused me to begin thinking about the differences between the British, the Irish, and the American languages and myths.

Wuthering Heights, Emily Brontë, captured my romantic imagination in adolescence and also instructed me that social class was important in fiction, no matter what American critics said.

The Second Sex, Simone de Beauvoir, I read when I was choking in an early marriage. It named feelings and ideas that I could not grasp without having a vocabulary in which to think about them and begin to discuss them.

A Prolegomena to the Study of Greek Religion, Jane Harrison, and **The Golden Bough**, James Frazer. I was led to Frazer by reading T.S. Eliot in high school, and Jane Harrison I came to from cultural anthropology my first year in college. Both taught me to think about tale and myth in ways I found fruitful and exciting, to see larger patterns, to link up story with the cultural and economic base.

U.S.A. by John Dos Passos. This was very important in showing an interesting way to combine traditional fictional form with the mass media.

MARGE PIERCY is a poet, essayist, and novelist. Her books of poetry include *Living in the Open*; *Stone, Paper, Knife*; and *Mars and Her Children*. Her novels include *Small Changes*; *Vida*; *Fly Away Home; Summer People;* and *He, She & It.*

WILLIAM H. PRITCHARD

Here is a list of five supremely funny 20th century satiric/comic novels by British and American writers:

Decline and Fall by Evelyn Waugh.
From a View to a Death by Anthony Powell.
Lucky Jim by Kingsley Amis.
Murphy by Samuel Beckett.
The Magic Christian by Terry Southern.

WILLIAM H. PRITCHARD is a professor of English at Amherst College. His books include *Seeing Through Everything: English Writers, 1918-1940; Frost: A Literary Life Reconsidered*; and *Randall Jarrell*. He edited the *Norton Anthology of American Literature.*

JUDITH ROSSNER

Grace Paley, **The Little Disturbances of Man**
Tillie Olsen, **Tell Me a Riddle**
Daniel Boorstin, **Landmark History of the American People** (2 volumes)
M.F.K. Fisher, **The Art of Eating**
Jakob Wasserman, **The Maurizius Case**

JUDITH ROSSNER is a novelist. Her books include *Looking for Mr. Goodbar*, *Attachments*, *August*, and *His Little Women*.

JOHN UPDIKE

Fiction comes in many books, none of them totally uninstructive. But let me name five that have meant a lot to me:

Don Quixote by Cervantes.
The Princess of Cleves by Madame de Lafayette.
Elective Affinities by Goethe.
Remembrance of Things Past by Marcel Proust.
Ulysses by James Joyce.

JOHN UPDIKE writes novels, short stories, poetry, and criticism. His novels include *The Centaur*, which received the National Book Award, *Rabbit Is Rich*, which received the Pulitzer Prize, and *The Witches of Eastwick.*

NIKKI GIOVANNI ON POETRY

Nothing more than an insatiable curiosity combined with an illogical and total empathy about, for, and with human beings is necessary to make a poet. I don't believe any three, five, or thousand books are indispensable but I have found three poets to whom I turn for humane qualities when I find my spirit lagging:

Langston Hughes. From **The Negro Speaks of Rivers**, written during his teen years, to his quintessential question: What happens to a dream deferred?, this leader of the Harlem Renaissance brought forth with love, humor, and understanding the beauty and strength of Black Americans.

Gwendolyn Brooks. Though Miss Brooks won the Pulitzer Prize for **Annie Allen**, my favorite books are **A Street in Bronzeville** and **In the Mecca**. She brings such wonderful imagery to a single line: This is the urgency: Live! What a charge to give to the inhabitants of *Nowhere with Nothing.*

Margaret Walker. The author of the award-winning **For My People** showed us younger poets that we could have political concerns and poetry; that we could integrate the personal with the political and still have art.

But mostly I believe a poet must master her own views of the world. We should be able to learn from anything and at any time. We should stand ready to engage both intellectually and emotionally with the very messy situation we call life.

NIKKI GIOVANNI is a poet and essayist. Her books of poetry include *Black Feeling, Black Talk, Black Judgement; The Women and the Men;* and *Those Who Ride the Night Winds.*

LIZ ROSENBERG ON POETRY

The Norton Anthology of Poetry and **The Norton Anthology of Modern Poetry**, however imperfect, are the most generous and complete collections of poetry written in the English language. Both contain more than a thousand pages of poetry, over one hundred poets.

The Voice that Is Great Within Us, edited by Hayden Carruth, is a very useful and eclectic anthology of 20th century American poetry.

Western Wind, edited by John Frederick Nims, and **The Norton Introduction to Poetry** are helpful as well, acting as introductions and guides to the art of poetry.

To find the great body of poetry written in languages other than English, one searches all one's life for individual books and poets. I'll list just a few: **Pindar**, **Sappho**, **Dante**, **Kenneth Rexroth**'s beautiful translations of Chinese and Japanese poems. Also **Rilke**, **Lorca**, **Baudelaire**, **Tagore**, **Akhmatova**, **Yevtushenko**, **Milozsh**, **Hikmet**. We Americans desperately need a good anthology of international poetry, and our lack of such a book speaks sadly for our condition.

For an understanding of American poetry and free verse, no book is more vital than Walt Whitman's **Leaves of Grass**.

To hear contemporary American poets thinking, arguing aloud about poetry, **Claims for Poetry** is a remarkable book, edited by poet/critic Donald Hall.

To understand the source of poetry and the poetic gift, I recommend Lewis Hyde's beautiful and thoughtful book-length essay, **The Gift**. In fact this book is so fine, so wide-ranging, so useful, sane, and generous in spirit, one may safely recommend it to anyone who lives and thinks.

LIZ ROSENBERG teaches poetry at the State University of New York at Binghamton. She is the author of *The Angel Poems* and *The Fire Music*.

MICHAEL HOLROYD ON BIOGRAPHY

Brief Lives by John Aubrey. These exotic glimpses into the late 16th and 17th centuries owe more to scholarly gossip than pedestrian research. But Aubrey's passionate curiosity about human nature gives these maverick lives their enduring vividness.

The Lives of the English Poets by Samuel Johnson. By turning readers' attention from vulgar public ambition towards domestic privacies, Johnson established biography as a discipline independent of history.

The Life of Samuel Johnson by James Boswell. Boswell was a great diarist and this biography of Johnson comes wonderfully alive whenever the two friends appear together on the page.

Eminent Victorians by Lytton Strachey. Strachey was a miniaturist and iconoclast who revolutionized the art of biography in the 20th century with his attack on 19th-century evangelicism, humanitarianism, education, and imperialism.

James Joyce by Richard Ellmann. A humane and sophisticated interlacing of life and work which marks the maturity of modern biography.

Footsteps by Richard Holmes. This subtle blending of biography, autobiography, and travelogue by a most adventurous biographer extends the range of biography and suggests a way in which it may develop in the future.

I was much influenced many years ago by Hugh Kingsmill's **The Progress of a Biographer**, which helped to make me a biographer, and for which I still retain admiration and affection.

MICHAEL HOLROYD is a biographer. His books include *Hugh Kingsmill*, *Lytton Strachey*, *Augustus John*, and *Bernard Shaw*.

JUSTIN KAPLAN ON BIOGRAPHY

You'll find some fiction listed here that dramatizes a challenge to biography as an independent literary genre.

Samuel Johnson, **Richard Savage** in *Lives of the English Poets*
James Boswell, **The Life of Samuel Johnson**
Henry James, **The Aspern Papers**
Lytton Strachey, **Eminent Victorians**
Virginia Woolf, **Orlando**
A.J.A. Symons, **The Quest for Corvo**
Erik Erikson, **Young Man Luther**
Somerset Maugham, **Cakes and Ale**

JUSTIN KAPLAN is a biographer, editor, and critic. His books include *Mr. Clemens and Mark Twain*, for which he received the Pulitzer Prize and National Book Award; *Lincoln Steffens: A Biography*, and *Walt Whitman: A Life*, which also received the National Book Award.

TONY RANDALL ON THEATRE

My Life in Art and **An Actor Prepares** by Stanislavski. Read what the master himself wrote — not what his epigones wrote.

The Scenic Art by Henry James and **Our Theatres in the Nineties** by George Bernard Shaw. The only criticism worth reading — because it was written by artists.

The Fervent Years by Harold Clurman. The best American book on theatre.

TONY RANDALL is the founder of the National Actors Theater, a nonprofit company that presents classic drama. As an actor he has appeared in more than a dozen movies, including "Pillow Talk" and "Huckleberry Finn." He won an Emmy for his portrayal of Felix Unger on the television series "The Odd Couple."

WENDY WASSERSTEIN ON THEATRE

The Complete Works of Shakespeare. For the sweep.

The Cherry Orchard, **The Three Sisters**, and **The Sea Gull** by Chekhov. For the humanity and comedy.

Act One by Moss Hart. For the show biz.

The Fervent Years by Harold Clurman. For how it all comes together.

WENDY WASSERSTEIN is a playwright and essayist. Her plays include "Isn't It Romantic," "The Heidi Chronicles," which won the Pulitzer Prize for drama, and "The Sisters Rosensweig."

MICHAEL FEINSTEIN ON AMERICAN POPULAR MUSIC

This list is top heavy with Gershwin, but so am I. For anyone wanting to gain insight on the greatest era of popular song writing, these books combined create a portrait of much more than just the musical aspirations of the '20s and '30s. It is an arbitrary list in some ways, but sure to illuminate and entertain.

Lyrics on Several Occasions by Ira Gershwin.
A Smattering of Ignorance by Oscar Levant.
George Gershwin, edited and designed by Merle Armitage.
Tin Pan Alley by Isaac Goldberg.
The World of Musical Comedy by Stanley Green.
The Gershwin Years by Edward Jablonski and Lawrence D. Stewart.
Passport to Paris by Vernon Duke.

MICHAEL FEINSTEIN is a leading interpreter of American popular music. He has had three extended runs on Broadway and has toured Europe with Liza Minnelli. His albums include "Pure Gershwin," "Michael Feinstein Sings Irving Berlin," and "Isn't It Romantic."

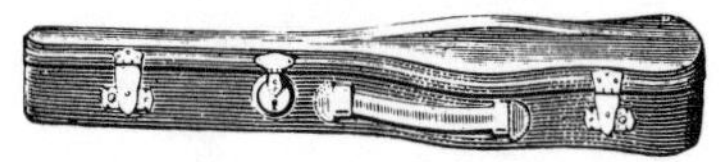

JACK FLAM ON ART

The best-written short history of Western art is E.H. Gombrich's **The Story of Art**. H.W. Janson's **History of Art** and recent editions of Helen Gardner's **Art Through the Ages** are less readable but are useful for the broader overviews they give, and especially for their illustrations.

Erwin Panofsky's **Meaning in the Visual Arts** is a stimulating collection of seminal essays by a great art historian and a remarkable thinker.

Heinrich Wölfflin's **Principles of Art History**, first published in 1915, still offers a compelling model for dealing with broad definitions of style and for its crucial notion of "a history of art without names."

Panofksy's **Early Netherlandish Painting** is a paradigm among studies of a single historical period. It can be read with pleasure and profit even by people who think they couldn't possibly be interested in Netherlandish painting.

John Rewald's **The History of Impressionism** and **Post-Impressionism from Van Gogh to Gauguin** remain remarkable achievements, comprehensive and richly-woven historical narratives about a subject that almost everyone seems interested in.

Janheinz Jahn's **Muntu: The New African Culture** and Robert Farris Thompson's **African Art in Motion** give wonderfully vivid accounts of how African art and culture interact.

Rhys Carpenter's **The Esthetic Basis of Greek Art** is a short but pithy and stimulating book that not only provides a wonderful introduction to Greek art but casts light on the whole Western tradition.

A book that has had a special impact on the way I think about art and literature in general is Heinrich Zimmer's **The King and the Corpse**, which brilliantly probes the meanings of myths and folktales, constantly alert to the ways that they combine profundity with delight.

T.S. Eliot's **Four Quartets** is the modern poem that resonates in me most.

JACK FLAM is an art historian and critic. He is Distinguished Professor of Art History at Brooklyn College and at the Graduate Center at the City University of New York. His books and exhibition catalogs include *Matisse: The Man and His Art, 1868-1918; Motherwell;* and *Richard Diebenkorn: Ocean Park.*

A house is a machine for living in.
— Le Corbusier

ROBERT A. M. STERN ON ARCHITECTURE

Vincent Scully: **American Architecture and Urbanism** and **Architecture: The Natural and the Manmade**
John Ruskin: **Seven Lamps of Architecture**
Geoffrey Scott: **The Architecture of Humanism**
Spiro Kostof: **A History of Architecture: Settings and Rituals**
Andrea Palladio: **The Four Books of Architecture [Quattro libri dell'architettura]** translated from Italian by Isaac Ware
Robert Venturi: **Complexity and Contradiction in Architecture**
Le Corbusier: **Towards a New Architecture [Vers une**

Architecture], translated from French by Frederick Etchells

Frank Lloyd Wright: **An Autobiography: Frank Lloyd Wright**

Steen Eiler Rasmussen: **Experiencing Architecture**, translated from Danish by Eve Wendt

Vitruvius Pollio: **The Ten Books on Architecture [De Architectura]**, translated from Latin by Morris Hicky Morgan

ROBERT A.M. STERN is an architect and a proponent of the "American vernacular" style of architecture. He has primarily designed fine homes, his designs extending to landscaping and interiors as well. He created and hosted the documentary series "Pride of Place" about American architecture on PBS, and co-authored *New York 1900: Metropolitan Architecture and Urbanism, 1890-1915.*

CHAPTER 3
THE HUMANITIES AND SOCIAL SCIENCES

This chapter highlights books on the issues and processes that involve us individually as human beings with intellects and spirits, and collectively as members of society. Among the works noted on learning, religion, and sociology are Rousseau's *Émile*, Vincent Van Gogh's *Letters to Theo*, and Elizabeth David's *French Provincial Cooking* — typical examples of the disparate and provocative selections shared by the contributors to *The Reader's Companion*.

PETER ELBOW ON LEARNING

My own experiences with learning have convinced me of one thing: Learning is not a neat process of taking in information or ideas. Only after we know something, do we see its neatness, coherence, and rationality and are we given a crucial measure of control. The process of learning requires some loss of neatness, coherence, rationality, and even control. Learning is messy and roundabout.

The books I have chosen are ones that tend to do justice to the complexity and nonlinear nature of learning — and the fact that it is not purely a "rational" process....I would put it this way: Learning means trying to swallow things and also risking and enduring being swallowed by things. I'll start with two complementary books — perhaps the most interesting on my list:

Forms of Intellectual and Ethical Development in the College Years by William Perry and **Women's Ways of Knowing: The Development of Self, Voice and Mind** by Mary Field Belenky, Blythe McVicker Clincy, Nancy Rule Goldberger, and Jill Mattuck Tarule. William Perry and his associates studied and interviewed college undergraduates and came up with a rich and interesting model for the stages that people go through in learning and growing — moving from naive, black-and-white authoritarian thinker to a sophisticated learner, able to accept the absence of certainty but still commit oneself. Belenky and her associates point out that Perry's sample is entirely male. They interview women at various ages and locations and come up with a different model for women's intellectual growth — equally rich and interesting, and centering on the concept of developing a voice. Both books give fascinating and rich chunks of interviews along with extended and ambitious analysis of them. Both books are particularly valuable for showing how learning is not just a process of taking things in, but really intertwined with deeper and more interesting processes of human development.

Language and Learning by James Britton. A British researcher and teacher writes in clear humane prose about how deeply language and learning are intertwined — with countless good insights about both.

On Knowing: Essays for the Left Hand by Jerome Bruner. A collection of enticing essays by a psychologist who has studied the psychology of learning perhaps as much as anyone else. Insight about and testimony to the fact that the process of learning is complex and interesting.

The Lives of Children by George Dennison. Fascinating picture of a school for children whom schools neglect that conveys deep principles of learning and teaching better than almost any book I know.

Democracy and Education: An Introduction to the Philosophy of Education by John Dewey. A classic text about how we tend not to learn unless we believe in the purpose for learning, unless we have some control over functioning as part of a live, real social system.

Children's Minds by Margaret Donaldson. This is a crisply written account of multiple experiments showing that children can learn in many ways that Piaget said they could not.

On Not Being Able to Paint by Joanna Field. A quiet, understatedly profound autobiographical account by a British psychoanalyst of her inner voyage toward more alive and meaningful perception and drawing. A book about the necessity of the imagination — and about the inherent link between what we see and who we are. Could just as well be about writing or music.

Frames of Mind: The Theory of Multiple Intelligence by Howard Gardner. Important research on how there is not one "intelligence" (for example, musical intelligence, social intelligence, or bodily intelligence).

Focusing by Eugene Gendlin. A phenomenologist philosopher writes for the lay public about how to make use of "felt sense" — nonverbal knowledge that exists tacitly in the body and feelings.

Personal Knowledge: Toward a Post-Critical Philosophy by Michael Polanyi. Perhaps the single most important philosophical book for me. Shows how the knowledge humans use in all realms, even science, is not "objective" or proven; yet, it is not just subjective or purely relativistic either. He argues how knowledge can be trustworthy but is always crucially personal: we always put a part of ourselves into any act of knowing. Also, knowing is always a social or "convivial" process.

Pygmalion in the Classroom by Robert Rosenthal and Lenore Jacobson. If we want to learn, we better find teachers who believe in us and in our intelligence. This book summarizes the extraordinary and extensive research about how learning is influenced more than anything else by the expectations of teachers about students.

Mind in Society: The Development of Higher Psychological Processes by Lev Vygotsky. A Russian psychologist writes in accessible prose about how thinking is essentially social and linguistic. Where Britton and Vygotsky stress the role of language in all learning, Gendlin and Polanyi stress how learning is not all linguistic.

PETER ELBOW is a professor of English at the University of Massachusetts at Amherst. His books include *Writing Without Teachers*; *Embracing Contraries: Explorations of Learning and Teaching;* and *What is English?*

NEIL POSTMAN ON LEARNING

People in Quandaries by Wendell Johnson. This book helps people to understand how we confuse ourselves and create unnecessary pain through the use of language. Johnson was a thoroughly sane person.

Understanding Media by Marshall McLuhan. While the answers McLuhan provides are not to be trusted, the questions he raises are of the greatest possible import. Thus, if you read this book as a series of questions rather than answers, you are bound to understand better what is happening.

The Technological Society by Jacques Ellul. Although Ellul is repetitious and even at times hysterical, there is no book I know of that better describes the conditions, paradoxes, and dangers of the society we live in.

Education for What Is Real by Earl Kelley. Long out of print and not much read when it was in print, this concise book explains better than any other what education and learning are about, and why.

Democracy in America by Alexis de Tocqueville. Any American who wants to understand what is both best and worst in our civilization can do no better than to keep this book close by so that a few pages can be read every day.

NEIL POSTMAN is professor of communication arts at New York University. He is the author of *Amusing Ourselves to Death: Public Discourse in the Age of Show Business* and *Conscientious Objections.*

DIANE RAVITCH ON LEARNING

The books that I turn to again and again to help understand learning in the United States are these:

Arthur Bestor, **Educational Wastelands**
Raymond Callahan, **Education and the Cult of Efficiency**
Lawrence A. Cremin, **The Transformation of the School**
John Dewey, **Experience and Education**
W.E.B. Du Bois, **The Souls of Black Folk**
Richard Hofstadter, **Anti-Intellectualism in American Life**
Robert Hutchins, **The Conflict in Education in a Democratic Society**
Jean Jacques Rousseau, **Émile**

DIANE RAVITCH is an historian of American education whose books include *The Troubled Crusade: American Education 1945-1980*; *The Schools We Deserve: Reflections of the Educational Crises of Our Times*; and *What Do Our 17-Year-Olds-Know?* She served as Assistant Secretary of Education under President George Bush and is currently a visiting fellow at the Brookings Institute.

Innocence is ashamed of nothing.
—Jean Jacques Rousseau, *Émile*

THEODORE R. SIZER ON LEARNING

My suggestions for books concerning the understanding of learning would be the following: John Dewey's **Democracy in Education**, Lawrence Cremin's **Popular Education**, and Howard Gardner's **The Unschooled Mind**. These are excellent examples of thinking by the best minds struggling to comprehend how learning happens.

THEODORE R. SIZER is chairman of the Coalition of Essential Schools, a research institute at Brown University. He is also the author of *Horace's School.*

RICK RODERICK ON PHILOSOPHY

The Trial and Death of Socrates by Plato. This collection of dialogues (**Euthyphro**, **Apology**, **Crito**, **Phaedo**) are at the heart of Western humanist tradition. They are dramatic and beautiful as well as well-argued and philosophically brilliant.

Meditations on First Philosophy by René Descartes. The seminal work in modern philosophy; it is also dramatically written and executed with incredible philosophical skill.

Grounding for the Metaphysics of Morals by Immanuel Kant. The greatest expression of the ethical insights of the Enlightenment. It is a difficult, but indispensable, work.

On Liberty by John Stuart Mill. A magnificent defense of liberty that continues to influence our discussions of the legitimate grounds for state coercion.

The Communist Manifesto by Karl Marx. One of the books that is absolutely necessary for an understanding of the 20th century.

Discipline and Punish by Michael Foucault. A postmodern critic develops a powerful account of the origins of our institutions, calling into question their "humanistic" underpinnings.

Necessary Questions by Anthony Appiah. The best introduction to current philosophical approaches in the Anglo-American tradition.

Feminism and Human Nature by Allison Jagger. The classic of contemporary philosophic approaches to feminism.

RICK RODERICK teaches philosophy at Duke University. His books include *Habermas and the Foundations of Critical Theory* and *Fragments of Transgression.*

Wonder is the feeling of a philosopher,
and philosophy begins in wonder.
— Plato, *Theatetus*

RICHARD RORTY ON PHILOSOPHY

Meno, **Euthyphro**, **Apology**, **Crito**, and **Phaedo** by Plato. These five short dialogues are often collected under the title **The Last Days of Socrates**. They form the best introduction to the Western philosophical tradition; as Whitehead rightly said, the rest of Western philosophy is a series of footnotes to Plato.

Dialogues Concerning Natural Religion by David Hume. This 18th-century work is still the best introduction to the question: "Can human reason, unassisted by special revelation, demonstrate the existence of a benevolent and omnipotent God?"

Twilight of the Idols by Friedrich Nietzsche. This attack on Platonism and Christianity is one of the most influential philosophic works of recent times.

Essays by William James. Some of James's essays — in particular **The Will to Believe** (in defense of the right to have a religious faith) and **The Moral Philosopher and the Moral Life** — are succinct expressions of pragmatism, the only distinctive American philosophical movement.

Consciousness Explained by Daniel Dennett. A very good example of contemporary analytic philosophy, drawing on recent work in computer programming and neurology to give us a radically new notion of what consciousness is.

RICHARD RORTY teaches philosophy at the University of Virginia, where he is University Professor of the Humanities. His books, which have been widely translated, include *Philosophy and the Mirror of Nature* and *Contingency, Irony, and Solidarity.*

BARRY HOLTZ ON JUDAISM

General guides and reference works:

Joseph Telushkin, **Jewish Literacy**. An easy-to-read popular encyclopedia of Judaism and Jewish history.

Geoffrey Wigoder, **The Encyclopedia of Judaism**. The best one-volume "serious" encyclopedia available.

Jacob Neusner, **The Ways of Torah**. A short, incisive introduction to Jewish religion and culture.

Milton Steinberg, **Basic Judaism**. A classic popular introduction.

The Schocken Guide to Jewish Books, edited by Barry Holtz. Essays by 16 scholars and teachers on what books to read in virtually all areas of Jewish thought, history, religion, and culture.

BARRY W. HOLTZ is co-director of the Melton Research Center at the Jewish Theological Seminary of America. He is the author of *Finding Our Way: Jewish Texts and the Lives We Lead Today.*

MARTIN MARTY ON CHRISTIANITY

Here is my list of books which help in the understanding of Christianity. I take for granted the **Bible**. Then:

Augustine, **The Confessions of St. Augustine**. The prototype for later Christian, religious, and most secular self-examining autobiography.

Dietrich Bonhoeffer, **Letters and Papers from Prison**. Among the most eloquent testimonies of 20th century experience "under the cross" in a Nazi concentration camp.

Blaise Pascal, **Pensées**. Sentence- or paragraph-length reflections on the paradoxes of living, of Christian living.

Simone Weil, **Waiting for God**. An erratic, probing set of essays and letters on life between Judaism and Christianity in the modern setting.

MARTIN E. MARTY teaches religion at the University of Chicago's Divinity School, where he is Fairfax M. Cone Distinguished Service Professor. He is the author of more than two dozen books, including *A Short History of Christianity* and *Righteous Empire,* which won the National Book Award.

JACOB NEUSNER ON JUDAISM

If I wanted to read about Judaism, in the English language alone, and knew nothing at all about that religion, I would start not with its holy books but with the way in which contemporary writers represent what it means to believe in and practice Judaism.

This Is My God by Herman Wouk. A grand writer, who believes in and practices Judaism, leads you through the life of Judaism as it is lived in the here and now: what Judaism means to someone who lives it every minute.

God in Search of Man: A Philosophy of Judaism by Abraham J. Heschel. The best mind in this century's theology of Judaism spells out the intellectual foundations and structure of the beliefs of Judaism.

The Sabbath: Its Meaning for Modern Man by Abraham J. Heschel. Heschel's explanation of the holiness of the Sabbath and how it infuses everyday life, forming out of the wherewithal of the common world a cathedral in time to God's glory, shows in a concrete way what it means to practice Judaism.

The Source by James Michener. The master of history through narrative weaves a fictional story in such a way as to convey the majesty and sweep of the history of the Jewish people, from the beginnings to the present.

My Name Is Asher Lev by Chaim Potok. A classic of contemporary fiction, which captures in an immediate way the dynamics of "being Jewish" and practicing Judaism as a richly portrayed human life spins itself out. Any other novel by Potok serves just as well. His is the authentic voice and vision of living Judaism today.

What these five books have in common is that they are written to be read, not merely pointed to, and that many who have read them have been changed by them.

JACOB NEUSNER is Distinguished Professor of Religious Studies at the University of South Florida, and the author of more than 50 books on Judaism. His most notable books include *Invitation to the Talmud: A Teaching Book*; *Invitation to Midrash: The Working of Rabbinic Bible Interpretation*; and *Judaism: The Evidence of Mishnah.*

HENRI NOUWEN ON SPIRITUALITY

I don't have memories of any one major book except for the **Bible** which has profoundly influenced my life and thinking. Indeed, the Bible is the basis of my life, a book that I read every day and that has an increasing influence on me. I perceive the Bible more and more as the Word of God that deeply transforms my inner life and continues to deepen, broaden, and strengthen my spirit. If you would ask me which book of the Bible has most influenced me, it is, without any doubt, the Gospel of St. John.

There I have found the most intimate connections with my life, and there I con-tinue to find an inexhaustible source for life, for love, and for hope.

Besides the Bible, I have no other books to mention. What I do have to mention are writers, and the three writers who have influenced me very much are John Henry Newman, Thomas Merton, and Vincent Van Gogh. John Henry Newman was the most important writer during my time at the seminary. His sermons preached at Saint Mary's in Oxford before he became a Catholic always impressed me very deeply. His **Apologia pro vita sua** and his **Idea of a University** also had a great impact on me. And, finally, his distinction between real and notional assent set me on the mystical path.

Thomas Merton's works taken together had a profound influence on my thinking. His ability to bring concrete burning issues of the day in connection with the spiritual search affected me very much. I like his **Seeds of Contemplation**, his **Conjectures of a Guilty Bystander**, his **Sign of Jonas**, his **Zen and the Birds of Appetite**, and many others. More than any one of these books, it is his spirit and his way of approaching life that have influenced me deeply.

Then there is Vincent Van Gogh. His **Letters to Theo** has had a major impact on my life, not one or two of them, but all of them together, especially in the context of his paintings, which have increasingly affected my deeper emotional life. Although Vincent Van Gogh is certainly not a religious writer in the traditional sense of the word, for me he was a man whose spirit touched my spirit very deeply, and who brought me in touch with some aspects of the spiritual life that no formal spiritual writer ever did.

Besides these three authors, there is one more influence that I'd like to mention; that is the influence of the Hesychastic Tradition, the spiritual tradition of the Eastern Orthodox Church. These are the writings of the

Desert Fathers, the early monks of Mount Sinai, the monks who lived in the 10th century on Mount Athos, and the many monks who wrote in 19th century Russia. **The Philokalia** and **The Art of Prayer** are probably the most important expressions of this tradition. I have probably learned more about the spiritual life from this Eastern Orthodox tradition than from Western spiritual writers.

HENRI NOUWEN is a Catholic priest and a spiritual writer. He is the author of more than 25 books, including *The Wounded Healer*, *The Genesee Diary*, and *Life of the Beloved*. Nouwen has taught at Yale and Harvard, and currently shares his life with mentally handicapped people as pastor of Daybreak, a L'Arche Community in Toronto.

SAYYID MUHAMMAD SYEED ON ISLAM

The Meaning of the Holy Qur'an by Abdullah Yusuf 'Ali new edition with revised translation. This book has enabled interested readers of English, who do not have great proficiency in reading and comprehending Qur'anic Arabic, to greatly enrich their understanding of the meaning and the incomparable beauty and perfection of the Glorious Qur'an.

Islam by Isma'il R. Al Faruqi. This volume seeks to portray the beliefs, practices, institutions, and history of Islam from the inside — as its adherents see them.

Towards Understanding Islam by Abul A'la Maududi. It offers a simple exposition of the essential teachings of Islam; its approach to life, the articles of faith, its scheme of worship, and the social order which it envisages.

The Cultural Atlas of Islam by Isma'il R. and Lois Lamiya'al Faruq. This magnificent book presents the entire world view of Islam — its beliefs, traditions, institutions, and its place in the cultures in which it has taken root. It is a comprehensive introduction to the Islamic experience in history and the modern world.

The Eternal Message of Muhammad by`Abd-al-Rahman `Azzam. This books shows that Islam is essentially a social religion, recognizing neither nationalism nor racism.

Islam in Focus by Hammudah Abdalati. A book written in the U.S., it uses an approach that is really intelligible, a style that is living, and a frame of mind that is easily understandable to the English-speaking reader.

Islam: The Straight Path by John L. Esposito. A well-written introduction to the study of Islam as a living faith by a genuine Western scholar of Islam. It has been described as "an answer to every teacher's prayer for an informed and balanced introductory book on Islam."

SAYYID MUHAMMAD SYEED is the director of academic outreach at the International Institute of Islamic Thought in Herndon, Virginia. He is also editor in chief of the *American Journal of Islamic Social Science*s.

WENDY DONIGER ON MYTHOLOGY

James G. Frazer, **The Golden Bough**
Sigmund Freud, **The Interpretation of Dreams**
Johan Huizinga, **Homo Ludens**
Claude Levi-Strauss, **The Jealous Potter**
Paul Ricouer, **The Symbolism of Evil**
C.S. Lewis, the **Narnia books**, especially **The Silver Chair**
John Updike, **The Centaur**

WENDY DONIGER teaches at the University of Chicago's School of Divinity. She is the author of *Other Peoples' Myths*, and, with Yves Bonnefoy, the two-volume *Mythologies.*

MARY CATHERINE BATESON ON CULTURAL ANTHROPOLOGY

Here is a group of books that provide an introduction to cultural anthropology. Most of these are classics, which means they've been extensively debated and criticized, but they provide a breadth and sense of discovery which is harder to find in the more specialized texts.

Ruth Benedict, **Patterns of Culture**. Benedict originated the idea that societies differ not only in their institutions and technologies but in their pervasive style. She illustrates this with characterizations of several Native American cultures and one from the South Pacific.

Colin Turnbull, **The Forest People**. Turnbull's depiction of the pygmies of the Ituri Forest is a vivid and appealing portrait of the awe and affection felt by this foraging people for their equatorial forest home.

Marjorie Shostak, **Nisa**. This is ethnography through the portrait of an individual, a woman of the desert-living !Kung Bushmen.

Margaret Mead, **New Lives for Old**. Although less well-known than some of Mead's earlier works, this hopeful study of the Manus people in the Admiralties in transition from the Stone Age to the modern world presents one of the most important themes of contemporary anthropology, the study of change.

Carol Stack, **All Our Kin: Strategies for Survival in a Black Community**. Here we see the techniques of anthropology applied to an urban black community, showing the necessity of understanding any culture from within.

Hortense Powdermaker, **Stranger and Friend**. This is a book about doing fieldwork in very different settings, including Hollywood and in the American South before the Civil Rights movement.

Clifford Geertz, **Local Knowledge**. Geertz represents a modern reexamination of the nature of anthropological interpretation.

MARY CATHERINE BATESON is a professor of anthropology and English at George Mason University. Her books include *Structural Continuity in Poetry: A Linguistic Study of Five Pre-Islamic Odes*; *With A*

Daughter's Eye: A Memoir of Margaret Mead and Gregory Bateson; and *Composing A Life*.

Our faith in the present dies out
long before our faith in the future.
— Ruth Benedict

LIONEL TIGER ON ANTHROPOLOGY

Konrad Lorenz, **King Solomon's Ring**, a charming and oddly prescient description of the study of animals in nature, not in labs.

Elias Canetti, **Crowds and Power**, which avoided the sterility of too much social science and yet penetrated the reality of turbulent social behavior.

Robert Ardrey, **African Genesis**, scientifically quite out of date but a landmark exposition of the connection between biology and social science which is also a model of aggressive popular scientific exposition.

Adam Smith, **The Theory of Moral Sentiments**, which is a more thoughtful and serious book than the *Wealth of Nations* which gets all the ink, including of course from the economist Galbraith. Here Smith shows how the thrilling adventure of the Scottish Moralists could be translated into the operations of socioeconomic life. It has had less influence than *Wealth of Nations* obviously because people are more interested in money than morals.

Elizabeth David, **French Provincial Cooking**, a pleasure to read as well as to use, and a critical influence on many cooks because it so sweetly and informatively linked food and social life. A modern equivalent is Barbara Tropp's **The Art of Chinese Cooking**.

Finally, Patrick Süskind's **Perfume** is an extraordinary discussion of human sensory activity and is also, I think, an allegory about Hitler, the man who didn't smell bad to his fellow citizens.

LIONEL TIGER is a professor of anthropology at Rutgers University. His books include *Men in Groups; The Manufacture of Evil: Ethics, Evolution, and the Industrial System*; and *The Pursuit of Pleasure*.

TODD GITLIN ON SOCIOLOGY

Sociology is a hybrid territory (the very word is half Latin, half Greek), and so it is difficult to sort out the elements. Among the introductions I would single out:

C. Wright Mills, **The Sociological Imagination**. What's dated is dated, but most of it isn't.

David Riesman, **The Lonely Crowd**. Still the most astute book I know about the peculiarities of American society after Alexis de Tocqueville's *Democracy in America*.

Max Weber's essays, **Science as a Vocation** and **Politics as a Vocation**.
Clifford Geertz, **The Interpretation of Cultures**. Although technically anthropology, walks the line where all social studies meet.

So many books have had an impact on my life, I scarcely know where to start. So, by free association, in no particular order:

Walt Whitman, **Leaves of Grass**
Doris Lessing, **The Golden Notebook**
Albert Camus, **The Myth of Sisyphus** and **The Rebel**

TODD GITLIN is a professor of sociology at the University of California at Berkeley. His books include *Inside Prime Time*, *The Murder of Albert Einstein*, and *The Sixties: Years of Hope, Days of Rage*.

NATHAN GLAZER ON SOCIOLOGY

Alexis de Tocqueville, **Democracy in America** and **The Old Regime and the French Revolution**
Max Weber, **The Protestant Ethic and the Spirit of Capitalism**
Emile Durkheim, **Suicide**
David Riesman, **The Lonely Crowd**
Daniel Bell, **The Coming of Post-Industrial Society**
Seymour M. Lipset, **Political Man**

NATHAN GLAZER has taught sociology at Harvard University since 1969. He was a collaborator, with Reuel Dennéy, on David Reisman's *The Lonely Crowd.* He is the author, with Daniel P. Moynihan, of *Beyond the Melting Pot* and of *The Limits of Social Policy.*

ROBERT NISBET ON SOCIOLOGY

The Protestant Establishment by E. Digby Baltzell.
Social Organization by Charles H. Cooley.
Beyond the Melting Pot by Nathan Glazer and Daniel P. Moynihan.
The Human Group by George Homans.
The Death and Life of Great American Cities by Jane Jacobs.
Political Man by Seymour M. Lipset.
Middletown by Robert and Helen Lynd.
The Sociological Imagination by C. Wright Mills.
The Culture of Cities by Lewis Mumford.
People of Plenty by David Potter.
The Lonely Crowd by David Riesman.
Folkways by William Graham Sumner.
Street Corner Society by William Foote Whyte.

ROBERT NISBET is the Albert Schweitzer Professor Emeritus of the Humanities at Columbia University. Among his two dozen books in history and sociology are *The Social Bond: An Introduction to the Study of Society* and *The Sociological Tradition.*

CHAPTER 4
THE NATURE OF SOCIETY

When considering books on those institutions, associations, and traditions which both link and divide us as nearest neighbors or farflung cohabitants of the globe, Shakespeare shares the stage with James Baldwin and Simone de Beauvoir. Imagine the compelling contemporary debate in which these writers might engage on the nature of society.

JONATHAN KOZOL ON RACISM AND POVERTY

An American Dilemma by Gunnar Myrdal.
Simple Justice by Richard Kluger.
Bearing the Cross by David Garrow.
Parting the Waters by Taylor Branch.

All of these important books remind us of the great unresolved tragedy of racial segregation and the grave inequalities that persist even today.

JONATHAN KOZOL taught in public school before turning to writing about children and poverty. He is the author of *Death at an Early Age,* which won the National Book Award, *Rachel and Her Children*, which won the Robert F. Kennedy award, and *Savage Inequalities*.

LEWIS LAPHAM ON SOCIETY

Shakespeare's plays, especially **King Lear**, **As You Like It**, **Antony and Cleopatra**, **Hamlet**, **The Tempest**, and **Henry IV, Part One**
Ford Maddox Ford, **The Good Soldier**
Edith Wharton, **The House of Mirth**
Charles Dickens, **The Pickwick Papers**
Herbert Jay Muller, **The Uses of the Past**
G.K. Chesterton, **The Collected Works**
The Letters of Henry Adams
Diderot, **Rameau's Nephew**
Flaubert, **Sentimental Education**
Ambrose Bierce, **The Devil's Dictionary**

LEWIS LAPHAM is editor of *Harper's* magazine and host of "Bookmark," a weekly public television series. His books include *Money and Class in America* and *Imperial Masquerade*.

My library was dukedom large enough.
— William Shakespeare, *The Tempest*

FRANCES FOX PIVEN ON POVERTY

From the Depths: The Discovery of Poverty in the United States by Robert H. Bremner. Still a good history of America's changing responses to poverty.

In the Shadow of the Poorhouse by Michael Katz. An up-to-date history of poverty in the United States, and our changing understanding of it.

The Other America by Michael Harrington. This book is said to have heralded the new awareness of poverty in the 1960s.

Tally's Corner by Elliot Liebow. A sensitive account of the impact of unemployment and poverty on self-esteem and family relations.

Blaming the Victim by William Ryan. An examination of the way we think about the poor.

Losing Ground by Charles Murray. This is the pithy, if inaccurate, conservative bible.

FRANCES FOX PIVEN is Distinguished Professor of Political Science at the City University of New York Graduate Center. She is co-author of *Regulating the Poor*, *Poor People's Movements*, and *Why Americans Don't Vote*.

PETER HALL ON URBAN CULTURE

The Culture of Cities by Lewis Mumford. This 1938 classic is still one of the most powerful and passionate analyses of urban history ever written, and also contains Mumford's vision of a future regional city structure for America. For this reason, it is still to be preferred to his 1961 rewriting, *The City in History*, though the latter also contains much of his most powerful writing.

The Urban Wilderness by Sam Bass Warner. This is a classic history of urban America, essential to all those wanting to understand why the American city has evolved in special ways that make it different from its European forebears.

The Contested City by John Mollenkopf. This 1983 study is a classic analysis of the forces that control American cities, and in particular gives a unique understanding of the ways in which civic boosterism has rebuilt urban economies.

The Truly Disadvantaged by William Julius Wilson. This 1987 study by a leading sociologist from the University of Chicago develops a striking thesis: that an urban underclass has evolved in American cities because of the collapse of basic industries and the out-migration of minority middle-class members to the suburbs. It is essential reading for those who want to understand the plight of the American inner city.

The Informational City by Manuel Castells. In this striking analysis, Manuel Castells argues that the modern economy has made a fundamental shift from manufacturing to the processing of information, as fundamental as the shift from agriculture to industry 200 years ago. He traces in detail the implications for urban work and urban life.

The Global City by Saskia Sassen. This book develops the thesis that service economy is now the fundamental fact of urban life, and shows the implications of working and living in three of the greatest global cities — New York, London, and Tokyo.

PETER HALL is director of the Institute of Urban and Regional Development at the University of California at Berkeley. He is also the author of *The World Cities.*

JACK NEWFIELD ON URBAN CULTURE

How the Other Half Lives by Jacob Riis. This was the first great book about urban, immigrant America, published in 1890. It gives an historical perspective on slums and the lifestyles of poor immigrants that helps place today's problems in context. It is muckraking with a novelist's eye and a poet's heart.

The Power Broker by Robert Caro. This is like *Moby Dick* and New York is the white whale. It is an investigative history of a city, and within it are nugget biographies of its leaders like Al Smith, Jimmy Walker, LaGuardia, FDR, and the autocratic Robert Moses.

Boss by Mike Royko. This is how politics really worked, told through the prism and personality of a popular but backward leader.

The Promised Land by Nicholas Lemann. This, too, offers the enlightening context of history to today's problems. It shows the impact of the migration of rural blacks to urban Chicago, and the cultural trauma of that transition.

A Tale of Two Cities by Charles Dickens. This classic still tells more than the Kerner Commission Report about wealth and poverty, envy and selfishness.

The Autobiography of Malcolm X as told to Alex Haley. A classic.

JACK NEWFIELD is the author of five books, including *The Permanent Government*, *City for Sale*, and *Robert Kennedy: A Memoir*. He has won the George Polk Award for political journalism and is currently a columnist for *The New York Post*.

AMIRI BARAKA ON RACE AND REVOLUTION

The Narrative of the Life of Frederick Douglass by Frederick Douglass.

Critical Remarks on the National Question by V.I. Lenin.

Black Reconstruction in America by W.E.B. Du Bois.

Good Morning Revolution by Langston Hughes.

Four Essays in Philosophy by Mao Tse-tung.

Big White Fog by Theodore Ward.

The Autobiography of Malcolm X as told to Alex Haley.
This Is My Century by Margaret Walker.

These books, which are painfully wrenched out of a much longer list, are what I would call the core of my concerns.

Douglass describes the real America and black life here from its inception and infers its legacy. Lenin sums up the question of the struggle of nations for self-determination and connects national struggle with socialist revolution.

Du Bois has written the greatest book of American history I know of. It explains exactly why we are where we are today. And the Sisyphus syndrome of black life in America.

Good Morning Revolution is Langston Hughes's revolutionary poems, the ones that got him in trouble. And some illuminating essays.

Mao's *Four Essays* is a fresh reading of dialectics and the philosophical science of revolution.

"Big White Fog," a great play summing up black nationalism and the Garvey Movement, expertly rendered in the ideological contrast of a black family in the '20s.

The Autobiography of Malcolm X is must reading because it sums up the second half of the 20th century vis-à-vis black life in America, just as Douglass did for the 19th.

The great Margaret Walker, the major living American poet, poetically sums up and characterizes the turbulent America she has witnessed.

AMIRI BARAKA is a writer and a professor of Afro-American Studies at the State University of New York at Stony Brook. His books of poetry include *Black Magic*, *Afrikan Revolution*, and *Reggae or Not!*. His plays include "Dutchman" and "Four Black Revolutionary Plays: All Praises to the Black Man." His other books include *Blues People: Negro Music in White America*; *The Autobiography of LeRoi Jones/Amiri Baraka*; and *The LeRoi Jones/Amiri Baraka Reader.*

CHANG-LIN TIEN ON ASIAN-AMERICANS

Ronald T. Takaki, **Strangers from a Different Shore**
Sucheng Chan, **This Bittersweet Soil: The Chinese in California Agriculture, 1860-1910.**

CHANG-LIN TIEN is the first Asian-American to hold the post of Chancellor of the University of California at Berkeley. Before becoming Chancellor in 1990, Tien was a professor of mechanical engineering. He was born in Wuhan, China, and came to the United States in 1956.

KENNETH B. CLARK ON RACE RELATIONS

An American Dilemma by Gunnar Myrdal is a fundamental analysis of the complexities of American race relations. It stimulated a major social science analysis of this problem.
The Negro Family in the United States by E. Franklin Frazier. Frazier wrote an objective approach to the sociological conflict and insights of American race relations.
From Slavery to Freedom: A History of Negro Americans by John Hope Franklin. As an historian, John Hope Franklin contributed an historical understanding,

bringing the events up to the present.

Race Differences by Otto Klineberg. Klineberg provided a major perspective to the psychological comparisons of racial groups.

KENNETH B. CLARK is a psychologist. His pioneering work on the effects of segregation was cited in the United States Supreme Court's *Brown v. Board of Education* decision. He is the author of *Dark Ghetto.*

MORRIS DEES ON RACE RELATIONS

Lay Bare the Heart: An Autobiography of the Civil Rights Movement by James Farmer.

My Soul Is Rested: The Story of the Civil Rights Movement in the Deep South by Howell Raines.

Nobody Knows My Name by James Baldwin.

Parting the Waters: America in the King Years 1954-63 by Taylor Branch.

Selma, 1965: The March that Changed the South by Charles E. Fager.

Voices of Freedom: An Oral History of the Civil Rights Movement from the 1950s through the 1980s by Henry Hampton and Steve Fayer.

We Are Not Afraid: The Story of Goodman, Schwerner, and Chaney and the Civil Rights Campaign for Mississippi by Seth Cagin and Philip Dray.

MORRIS DEES has served as the chief trial counsel for the Southern Poverty Law Center in Montgomery, Alabama, since 1971. He is the author of *Season for Justice: The Life and Times of Civil Rights Lawyer Morris Dees.*

MICHAEL DORRIS ON NATIVE AMERICANS

Francis Jennings, **The Invasion of America**
Louise Erdrich, **Love Medicine**
James Welch, **Winter in the Blood**
Angie Debo, **A History of the Indians of the United States**
Nancy Lurie, editor, **Mountain Wolf Woman**

MICHAEL DORRIS is a professor of anthropology and Native American studies at Dartmouth College. His books include *The Broken Cord*, *A Yellow Raft in Blue Water*, and *The Crown of Columbus*, with Louise Erdrich; and *Working Men: Stories.*

EUGENE D. GENOVESE ON AFRICAN-AMERICANS

From Slavery to Freedom by John Hope Franklin. Still by far the best introduction to Afro-American history, with the additional strength of having excellent comparative selections on Africa and Latin America.

Reconstruction After the Civil War by John Hope Franklin. A small book that provides a good overview of the black experience during Reconstruction.

Souls of Black Folk by W.E.B. Du Bois. I cannot imagine a course without a slice of Du Bois, and this is an especially searing piece of work.

Black Reconstruction in America by W.E.B. Du Bois. Tendentious and controversial, but a seminal work.

Water from the Rock by Sylvia Frey. The best study of blacks in the Revolutionary era.

There Is a River by Vincent Harding. An interpretive history of blacks up to the Civil War, written from a "black nationalist" point of view. However controversial, it is a responsible work of scholarship, brilliantly written.

Black Culture and Black Consciousness by Lawrence Levine. The best introduction to black culture in America I know of.

Slavery and Freedom on the Middle Ground by Barbara Fields. Although a study of Maryland, this is a first-class book on the transition from slavery to freedom: careful scholarship, social history integrated with political and economic history, a brilliant analysis.

Within the Plantation Household by Elizabeth Fox-Genovese. Although more on white women on the slave plantations than black women, it is the best work yet on the latter. But the author is my wife, so I may be prejudiced.

Down by the Riverside by Charles Joyner. An intense study of slave life in one community by an author trained as a folklorist as well as a historian.

This Species of Property: Slave Life and Culture in the Old South by Leslie Owens. Among many fine studies of slave life in the South, as a whole, this may well be the best.

Slave Religion by Albert Raboteau. Religion played a crucial role in black life, and this book is a fine introduction to its salient features.

Been in the Storm So Long by Leon Litwack. The transition from slavery to freedom across the South.

Branches Without Roots by Gerald Jaynes. The finest work on the economic aspects of the transition from slavery to freedom.

Frederick Douglass — choose from the number of versions of his autobiographical writings, supplemented with William McFeeley's recent biography of Frederick Douglass.

Negro Thought by August Meier. On the response of blacks to the problems of the post-Reconstruction era — Booker T. Washington, the early Du Bois, et al.

A comparative focus is indispensable. I would recommend **Slavery and Human Progress** by David Brion Davis as an introduction to slavery in the history of **Western Civilization; Race and Slavery in the Middle East** by Bernard Lewis to combat much fashionable nonsense; and **Transformations in Slavery** by Paul Lovejoy on what slavery in Africa really looked like.

EUGENE D. GENOVESE teaches history at Emory University, and is the author of *The Political Economy of Slavery* and *The World the Slaveholders Made.*

To be a poor man is hard, but to be a poor race in a land of dollars is the very bottom of hardships.
— W. E. B. Du Bois, *The Souls of Black Folk*

LADONNA HARRIS ON NATIVE AMERICANS

Indian Givers and **Native Roots** by Jack Weatherford.
Love Medicine and other books by Louise Erdrich.
The Conquest of Paradise: Christopher Columbus and the Columbian Legacy by Kirkpatrick Sale.

Each of these books presents a positive and alternative view of the contributions of American Indians to both the past and to contemporary America.

LADONNA HARRIS is executive director of Americans for Indian Opportunity, an organization dedicated to strengthening tribal governments and native rights advocacy. She helped found the National Women's Political Caucus.

JAMAKE HIGHWATER ON NATIVE AMERICANS

The Trial by Franz Kafka, which illuminated the dark realities of people (minorities and otherwise) who live on the margins of an authoritarian society.

To the Lighthouse by Virginia Woolf, which taught me a great deal about the virtues of visionary, nonlinear literature by comparison to the overly applauded realist style of the dominant Western society.

The Next Development in Man by L.L. Whyte, which verified my hope that there is more than one reality and that there is, therefore, a vindication of the realities of peoples who live outside the Western mindset.

Problems of Art and **Philosophy in a New Key** by Susanne K. Langer, which clarified the importance of virtual reality and the existence of a metaphoric mentality equal to the predominant rational point of view.

The Hero with a Thousand Faces by Joseph Campbell, which helped me to understand as a young man that there are advantages in being an outsider.

Three Tragedies by Federico García Lorca, which gave me hope of finding a literary voice capable of expressing a vision that grows out of my own ethnicity and my own mythology.

JAMAKE HIGHWATER is a writer whose books include *Song from the Earth: American Indian Painting*; *Anpao: An American Indian Odyssey*; *The Primal Mind: Vision and Reality in Indian America*; and *Myth and*

Sexuality. He has directed various festivals, including the 1986 Native Arts Festival in Houston and the 1991 Festival Mythos in Philadelphia.

ELLWYN R. STODDARD ON HISPANIC AMERICANS

Dictionary of Mexican American History, edited by Matt S. Meier and Feliciano Rivera. By alphabetized item or name, the most relevant aspects of Mexican American history are covered as a succinct summary.

Borderlands Sourcebook, edited by Ellwyn R. Stoddard, Richard L. Nostrand, and Jonathan P. West. An encyclopedic assortment of bibliographical summaries of all aspects of border life and institutions, from archeological surveys to current migration, drug traffic, and education.

Spain in America by Charles Gibson. A hard-hitting approach which penetrates the "European-superiority myths" of conquest and objectively shows how European racism and ethnocentrism became implanted in the New World.

Mexico: The Struggle for Modernity by Charles C. Cumberland. A penetrating examination of the early establishment of institutions in Meso-America and Mexico.

Race Mixture in the History of Latin America by Magnus Mörner. A small monograph, well-documented, showing the preservation of racism and privilege in Spanish-dominated Latin and Central America.

A Documentary History of the Mexican Americans, edited by Wayne Moquin. Lesser known letters and documents, along with truly insightful introductions, all of which show the relationships of missions to Indians, presidios to missions, etc., and cut through the sticky-sweet myths of current "whitewashed" histories.

Border: The U.S.-Mexico Line by Leon C. Metz. A true delight to read (Metz is a fine storyteller), this book is very well-documented and extremely accurate as it leads the reader through the historical maze of events and people who created this region.

From Peones to Politicos: Ethnic Relations in a South Texas Town, 1900-1977 by Douglas E. Foley, Clarice Mota, Donald E. Post, and Ignacio Lozano. An "ol' boy" ethnography from the Hispanics who suffered through racism and exploitation in South Texas and the Lower Rio Grande Valley.

El Paso: A Borderlands History by W.H. Timmons. A very balanced and well-documented analysis of the development of this critical region.

The Indian Heritage of America by Alvin M. Josephy, Jr. The best and most readable account of Native American groups throughout the U.S., showing their diversity and institutional relationships with their resources.

Cycles of Conquest by Edward H. Spicer. An articulate view of pre-European peoples of the Southwest who were conquering each other and being taken captive by other Indian groups as the power shifted from one group to another. Excellent focus on the Southwest where most Mexican Americans have grown up.

ELLWYN R. STODDARD is a professor of sociology and anthropology at the University of Texas at El Paso. He is the author of *Mexican Americans* and *Patterns of Poverty Along the U.S.-Mexico Border* (with John Hedderson).

GARY BAUER ON FAMILIES

A Death in the Family by James Agee. Movingly written story of how a father's accidental death affects the family he leaves behind — somber, but leaves an indelible impression of love and family life.

Surprised by Joy by C.S. Lewis. A handbook on surviving an English public education and rediscovering a spiritual dimension after flirtations with the inadequate substitutes for God in the 20th century — art, science, and politics.

The Diary of a Young Girl by Anne Frank and **The Hiding Place** by Corrie Ten Boom. Both are about families in the shadow of absolute evil.

A Christmas Carol by Charles Dickens. Dickens understood the role of families in curing (and, when they break down, causing) social ills.

Brideshead Revisited by Evelyn Waugh. Christian faith, rediscovered through family ties, vanquishes human vanities.

GARY L. BAUER is president of the Family Research Council. He was formerly Undersecretary of Education and Assistant to the President for Policy Development and Chairman of the White House Working Group on the Family under President Reagan. He is the author of *Our Journey Home* and, with James C. Dobson, of *Children at Risk*.

ROBERT COLES ON THE FAMILY

Tolstoy's **War and Peace**
George Eliot's **Middlemarch**
Tillie Olsen's **Tell Me a Riddle**
William Carlos Williams: **White Mule**; **In the Money**; and **The Build-Up**
Raymond Carver's **Where I'm Calling From**

All of these novels and stories evoke the complexities of this life we live — alone and together as members of families, of a community. I find that fiction does more justice to life's subtleties, nuances, and ironies than social science!

ROBERT COLES is a child psychiatrist and author of more than 25 books. He has been a research psychiatrist at the Harvard University Health Services since 1963. His books include the Pulitzer Prize-winning *Children of Crisis*, *The Call of Stories*, and *The Spiritual Life of Children*.

ELLEN GALINSKY ON THE FAMILY

Children of Crisis (5 volumes) by Robert Coles. A compelling portrait of the strength of children under crisis.

Vulnerable but Invincible by Emmy Werner and Ruth Smith. A fascinating study of how children fare under difficult life circumstances — who does well, who doesn't, and why.

Surviving the Breakup: How Children and Parents Cope with Divorce by Judith S. Wallerstein and Joan Berlin Kelly. A small but eloquent study of the impact of divorce.

Within Our Reach by Lisbeth B. Schorr. A study of successful programs that prevent family problems or help families with difficulties.

The Second Shift by Arlie Hochschild. A vivid and important study of women's and men's lives when both parents work.

The Measure of Our Success by Marian Wright Edelman. An open letter to all those who care about children.

And a book that deeply affected me personally is **The Magic Years** by Selma Fraiberg. It offers unusual insight into how children experience their world. This is a portrait, however, that leaves out parents and their perspectives. In reaction to this book in part, I wrote *The Six Stages of Parenthood* and *The Preschool Years,* which I meant to bring both parents' and children's development in focus.

ELLEN GALINSKY is co-president of the Families and Work Institute, a research organization, and a former faculty member of the Bank Street College of Education. Her books include *The New Extended Family: Day Care that Works*; *The Six Stages of Parenthood*; and *Beyond the Parental Leave Debate.*

MARGARET KUHN ON AGING

Why Survive?: Being Old in America by Dr. Robert N. Butler. Butler's book won a Pulitzer Prize for its perceptive analysis of widely held myths about old age and the process of aging. His positive analysis of aging and the demographic revolution has influenced policy and practice in our changing society.

The Aging Enterprise by Carroll L. Estes. Estes describes the burgeoning number of programs and services set up to respond to the needs of older Americans, and observes that our society had to declare old age a problem to make the gross national product grow. Her book raises urgent questions about empowerment and the role and status of women in late life. It is a book to read and quote!

MARGARET KUHN founded the Gray Panthers on her 65th birthday in 1970. As head of the organization, Kuhn has sought to eradicate "ageism." She is the author of several books, including *Maggie Kuhn on Aging*; *No Stone Unturned: The Life and Times of Maggie Kuhn*; and *You Can't Be Human Alone.*

MARK GOLD ON DRUGS

Getting Tough on Gateway Drugs: A Family Guide by Robert Dupont. Any discussion or study of the initiation of illicit drug use or adolescent drug use begins with a discussion of cigarette, alcohol, and marijuana use. Dr. Dupont puts the drug use and addiction epidemic in perspective and gives readers new insight into early drug and alcohol use as necessary conditions for cocaine, narcotic, or other drug use. Educational and prevention efforts focused on "gateway drugs" offer concrete and workable steps in reducing use and addiction.

The Forgotten Children by M. Cork. The first and most compelling description of children of alcoholics. Now accepted as a very high risk group for problems of living and alcoholism, this pioneering book says it all with conviction.

The American Disease, revised edition, by David Musto. America is the leading drug-consuming nation, with an unprecedented appetite for opiates, cocaine, and marijuana. What are the roots of this fascination and the high rates of addiction we have today? Psychiatrist and historian Musto describes the historical roots and causes of our disease.

The Biochemical Basis of Neuropharmacology by Jack Cooper, Floyd Bloom, and Robert Roth. Classic reference text explains in clear terms the site of action for the drugs of abuse — the brain. Since drugs of abuse are taken to produce euphoria and avoid withdrawal and both are brain-mediated events, understanding the brain systems involved in drug action and withdrawal is essential.

Drug and Alcohol Abuse: A Clinical Guide to Diagnosis and Treatment by Marc A. Schuckit, 3rd edition. Each drug problem and treatment is described in sufficient detail and clarity to make this an indispensable reference for students and clinicians.

Substance Abuse: A Comprehensive Textbook by Joyce Lowinson, Pedro Ruiz, and Robert Millman, 2nd edition. This classic text brings together the best work from every established expert in a form which is clear and compelling.

Alcoholics Anonymous: The Story of How Many Thousands of Men and Women Have Recovered from Alcoholism, Alcoholics Anonymous World Services, 3rd edition. No reading list would be complete without a description of the treatment process which has helped the most people throughout the world become and stay abstinent. Alcoholics Anonymous is now the standard and model treatment for the detoxified adult.

DR. MARK GOLD is visiting professor of neuroscience and psychiatry at the University of Florida College of Medicine and formerly a faculty member at the Yale Medical School where he researched opiate drug addiction treatments. Dr. Gold founded the first national drug hotline in 1983 and served as an adviser to the Justice Department and the White House Office of Drug Policy. His books include *Wonder Drugs*; *Cocaine*; *Marijuana*; and *The Good News About Drugs and Alcohol: Curing, Treating, and Preventing Substance Abuse in the New Age of Biopsychiatry.*

LESTER GRINSPOON ON DRUGS

Substance Abuse: Clinical Problems and Perspectives, 2nd edition, Joyce Lowinson and Pedro Ruiz, editors. An encyclopedic reference work with sections on specific drugs as well as general articles on history, theory, and treatment.

Treating Drug Problems, Volume I: A Study on the Evolution, Effectiveness and Financing of Public and Private Drug Treatment Systems by the Institute of Medicine. The latest and best survey of the resources and effectiveness of existing drug treatment programs.

From Chocolate to Morphine: Understanding Mind-active Drugs and **The Natural Mind: A New Way of Looking at Drugs and the Higher Consciousness**, revised edition, by Andrew Weil and Winifred Rosen. Intelligent, well-written advice for consumers on the use and abuse of drugs, and the alternatives.

Dark Paradise: Drug Addiction in America Before 1940 by David T. Courtwright. A scholarly monograph that provides a model of careful, unprejudiced, historical research on a field that has seen very little of it.

Drug Use in America: Problem in Perspective (4 volumes) by the National Commission on Marihuana and Drug Abuse. The report of a federal commission in the era before the War on Drugs: outdated in part, but still more valuable than almost anything that has come from American official sources since.

Licit and Illicit Drugs: The Consumers Union Report on Narcotics, Stimulants, Depressants, Inhalants, Hallucinogens, and Marihuana — Including Caffeine, Nicotine, and Alcohol by Edward Brecher. An accurate and readable guide.

The Truth About Addiction and Recovery by Stanton Peele and Archie Brodsky. An interesting exploration of new models and proposals for drug treatment.

The Drug Legalization Debate, edited by James A. Inciardi. The issue that will not go away, discussed by a half dozen authors from various points of view.

LESTER GRINSPOON is an associate professor of psychiatry at Harvard University. He is the author of *Psychedelic Drugs Reconsidered*; *Drug Control in a Free Society*, with James Bakalak; and *Marihuana: the Forbidden Medicine.*

THOMAS SZASZ ON DRUGS

The Pharmacological Basis of Therapeutics by Louis Goodman and Alfred Gilman. The first edition of what has become the standard American textbook of pharmacology; a useful source concerning the pharmacological effects of currently illegal drugs, as yet unprejudiced by the Drug War hysteria.

The Drug Hang-Up: America's Fifty-year Folly by Rufus King. An excellent critique of drug controls by a prominent

Washington attorney.

Extraordinary Popular Delusions and the Madness of Crowds by Charles Mackay, 1841. A neglected, old classic on "crowd madnesses" through history, such as our War on Drugs.

On Liberty by John Stuart Mill. The classic statement on the individual's rights with respect to "self-regarding behavior" — that is, conduct (such as drug use) that may adversely affect the actor, but does not directly harm others.

Human Action: A Treatise on Economics by Ludwig von Mises. The modern classic on free market economics and philosophy, including the market in drugs.

Era of Excess: A Social History of the Prohibition Movement by Andrew Sinclair. An indispensable history of the folly and tragedy of statist drug controls, exemplified by Prohibition.

The Toadstool Millionaires: A Social History of Patent Medicines Before Federal Regulation by James Harvey Young. A useful, albeit biased, account (supporting statist, medical-paternalistic drug controls) of drug marketing and drug use in the United States before 1906.

DR. THOMAS SZASZ is a psychiatrist and an advocate for the legalization of drugs. He is the author of *The Myth of Mental Illness: Foundations of a Theory of Personal Conduct*; *Ceremonial Chemistry: The Ritual Persecution of Drugs, Addicts, and Pushers*; and *The Right to Drugs: The Case for a Free Market*. Dr. Szasz is professor emeritus of psychiatry at the State University of New York's Health Science Center in Syracuse.

HELEN GURLEY BROWN ON WOMEN

In a Different Voice by Carol Gilligan. A study of the moral issues confronting women.

Backlash by Susan Faludi. She shows just how far women haven't come in the last 15 years.

You Just Don't Understand by Deborah Tannen. This best-seller looks at how men and women speak different languages.

Fear of Flying by Erica Jong. Very old but quite mind-opening when it was first published.

Sexual Personae by Camille Paglia. Off-beat opinions about women's place in the world, and just about everything else she can think of.

How to Make an American Quilt by Whitney Otto. Connected stories about women in a quilting group.

The Feminine Mystique by Betty Friedan. Ancient but truly revolutionary.

Male and Female by Margaret Mead. She seemed to define rather clearly the differences between men and women in our culture and others.

HELEN GURLEY BROWN has been the editor of *Cosmopolitan* magazine since 1965. Her books include *Sex and the Single Girl*, *Having It All*, and *The Late Show*.

SAM KEEN ON MEN

Norman O. Brown, **Love's Body**
Glen Gray, **The Warriors**
Susan Griffin, **Pornography and Silence**
Gabrile Marcel, **The Mystery of Being**
Hannah Arendt, **The Human Condition**

SAM KEEN is a writer and lecturer on the philosophy of religion and psychology, and is the author of *Apology for Wonder, The Passionate Life: Stages of Loving*, and *Fire in the Belly: On Being a Man.*

FRANCES LEAR ON WOMEN

The Second Sex by Simone de Beauvoir. The birth of feminism.
The Feminine Mystique by Betty Friedan. The popularization of feminism.
The Diary of a Mad Housewife by Sue Kauffman. The personal need for feminism.
A Room of One's Own by Virginia Woolf. The artist's plea for feminism.
In a Different Voice by Carol Gilligan. The basis for feminine psychology.

FRANCES LEAR launched *Lear's* magazine in 1985, and serves as editor-in-chief. Her autobiography is *The 2nd Seduction.*

Women have served all these centuries as looking-glasses possessing the magic and delicious power of reflecting the figure of man at twice its natural size.
— Virginia Woolf, *A Room of One's Own*

LEONARD MICHAELS ON MEN

Hamlet, Shakespeare. What men feel about life and death.
Essays, Montaigne. What men think about virtually everything and how they discover their personal identity.
The Old Testament, various authors. How men behave.
The Republic, Plato. How men think at the highest and most abstract level, and what goodness and pleasure there is in thinking and talking as opposed to anything else.
Chekhov's stories. How men love and women love.

LEONARD MICHAELS teaches English at the University of California at Berkeley and is a writer. His many works include *To Feel These Things* and *The Men's Club*.

LETTY COTTIN POGREBIN ON WOMEN

The Second Sex by Simone de Beauvoir. This is the essential text without which no one can claim to understand the status and condition of women in Western societies in the 20th century.

Woman in Sexist Society: Studies in Power and Powerlessness, edited by Vivian Gornick and Barbara K. Moran. A richly rewarding anthology of essays analyzing women's roles, socialization, and oppression at the beginning of the Second Wave of the women's movement in America.

A Heritage of Her Own: Toward a New Social History of American Women, edited by Nancy F. Cott and Elizabeth H. Pleck. A feminist perspective on female experience in this country from the 17th century through the 20th century.

The Mermaid and the Minotaur: Sexual Arrangements and Human Malaise by Dorothy Dinnerstein. A dazzling theoretical exploration of the origins of men's resentment of women and the inevitability of patriarchy.

Against Our Will: Men, Women and Rape by Susan Brownmiller. The classic study of rape and its by-product: women's fear and powerlessness.

LETTY COTTIN POGREBIN is the author of seven books, including *Deborah, Golda, and Me: Being Female and Jewish in America*. She is a founding editor of *Ms.* magazine and has been a columnist for *The New*

York Times, *Ms.*, and *Moment* magazine. She lectures on women's issues and Middle East politics.

PEPPER SCHWARTZ ON MEN, WOMEN, AND SEX

I have been influenced by both fiction and nonfiction books. The following have really moved and motivated me:

The Future of Marriage by Jessie Bernard.
The Dialectic of Sex by Shulamith Firestone.
Sexual Conduct by Bill Simon and John Gaynor.
Portrait of a Marriage by Nigel Nicholson.
Sexual Behavior in the Human Male by Alfred C. Kinsey.
Sexual Politics by Kate Millett.
The Woman Warrior by Maxine Hong Kingston.
The Story of O by Pauline Reage.
Prince of Tides by Pat Conroy.
Fear of Flying by Erica Jong.
The poems of **Edna St. Vincent Millay**.

PEPPER SCHWARTZ is a professor of sociology at the University of Washington. She is the author, with Philip Blumstein, of *American Couples: Money, Work and Sex* and, with Judith Long Laws, of *Sexual Scripts: The Social Construction of Female Sexuality.*

MARTIN DUBERMAN ON GAY CULTURE

Intimate Matters: A History of Sexuality in America by John D'Emilio and Estelle Freedman.
Being Homosexual: Gay Men and Their Development by Richard Isay.
Christianity, Social Tolerance and Homosexuality by John Boswell.
One Hundred Years of Homosexuality by David Halperin.
Constraints of Desire by John Winkler.
Coming Out Under Fire: The History of Gay Men and Women in World War II by Allan Berube.
Odd Girls and Twilight Lovers by Lillian Faderman.

MARTIN DUBERMAN is an historian at the Graduate Center of the City University of New York and the author of *Cures: A Gay Man's Odyssey*. He also edited *Hidden from History: Reclaiming the Gay and Lesbian Past.*

CHAPTER 5
LIFESTYLE AND POPULAR CULTURE

It can be argued that what has become known as "popular culture" is the dramatic result of our increasingly media-dominated environment. What used to be the simple tastes, habits, and trends of a society now become national obsessions as millions of eyes search the horizon (or their computer network bulletin boards) for the next wave. In the immediate sense, it can be hard to keep up. But as the following booklists reflect, there are no end of great classics to be read on the "fun stuff"— sports, food, fitness, even humor.

ARTHUR ASHE ON SPORTS

Levels of the Game by John McPhee. Describes the personal lives of Arthur Ashe and Clark Graebner through the semi-final tennis match at the 1968 U.S. Open Tennis Championship.

SportsWorld: An American Dreamland by Robert Lipsyte. Describes the almost pathological hold of sports on the American psyche.

The Chrysanthemum and the Bat by Robert Whiting.

Describes the game of baseball from the American and Japanese perspectives. Fascinating!

Golf in the Kingdom by Michael Murphy. Describes a fictional round of golf in Ireland played by an American under the strictest of rules.

The Fight by Norman Mailer. Need I say more?

ARTHUR ASHE won many major tennis tournaments, including the U.S. Open, Australian Open, and Wimbledon. He was the author of *A Hard Road to Glory*, a history of the African-American athlete, and *Days of Grace*, a memoir. Mr. Ashe died in 1993.

ROGER KAHN ON BASEBALL

Pitching in a Pinch by Christy Mathewson. Mathewson, probably the first college graduate to ever star in the major leagues, and his uncredited ghost John Wheeler provide vivid portraits of the early game, early players, early umpires, early managers. And the book is truly fun to read.

The Glory of Their Times by Lawrence Ritter. An oral history, interviews with 22 ballplayers prominent in the first quarter of the century. Ritter sensibly edited his questions from the finished book. The best baseball oral history to date.

Veeck as in Wreck by Bill Veeck with Ed Linn. These are the almost complete confessions of baseball's Barnum, the most remarkable hustling promoter baseball has known. Veeck's the one who hired a midget to pinch hit. The midget walked. Serious, funny, and charming.

Baseball in America by Donald Honig. The best, if not the most scholarly, history of the game. The author brings ringing vitality to the legends, Nap Lajoie, Tris Speaker, Grover Cleveland Alexander.

The Long Season by Jim Brosnan. This is the diary of a single season spent as a relief pitcher for the Cardinals and Reds. He is literate, sensitive, aware and, when he gets a chance, a pretty damn good relief pitcher. He's conversational, sarcastic, hip. "All coaches," he writes, "carry fungo bats in the spring to ward off suggestions that they aren't working."

Willie's Time by Charles Einstein. My favorite biography. A memoir of the author, of 25 years and the great centerfielder. Big, complex, not without flaws, and wonderful.

Bang the Drum Slowly by Mark Harris. This is a novel, a story of an athlete dying young, told in baseball vernacular, derived from the style of Ring Lardner. It's the story of a pitcher and catcher, of young men growing up in a hurry in baseball and beyond. You will not soon forget the protagonist, Henry Wiggen.

The Natural by Bernard Malamud. Another novel. Mystical, somewhat heavy at times but — and I don't mean to sound pretentious — literature. If you know the symbolism, you're well ahead. If not, this is still memorable reading.

ROGER KAHN is the author of several award-winning books on baseball including *The Boys of Summer*, *The Seventh Game*, and *The Era: 1947-1957, When the Yankees, the New York Giants, and the Brooklyn Dodgers Ruled the World*. He was also president of the Utica Blue Sox, a minor league baseball team.

ROBERT LIPSYTE ON SPORTS

Jim Bouton (edited by Leonard Schecter), **Ball Four**. This valentine to the national pastime captures the essence of the game and its grip on players and fans.

Bill Bradley, **Life on the Run**. A smart, candid portrait of the pro basketball gypsy life by the future senator.

Howard Cosell (with Peter Bonventre), **I Never Played the Game**. The best of his memoir-screeds by the most important sports journalist of his time.

Robert Creamer, **Babe**. A splendid biography of the quintessential American celebrity jock-boy.

Harry Edwards, **The Struggle That Must Be**. A former scholarship athlete and sports militant, now a Berkeley professor and establishment consultant, unearths the roots of today's black athlete.

Paul Gallico, **A Farewell to Sport**. This journalist's memoirs are a fascinating and readable impression of early 20th century sport and its gender and racial biases.

Harvey Green, **Fit for America**. Health, fitness, and sport in American society.

Allen Guttmann, **Women's Sports: A History**. A respected historian offers a solid academic document.

Thomas Hauser, **Muhammad Ali**. A wonderful oral history of the people around the most influential athlete of this century.

Jerome Holzman, **No Cheering in the Pressbox**. A delightful, myth-shattering series of interviews with the leading sportswriters of the first half of the 20th century

David Kopay and Perry Deane Young, **The David Kopay Story**. A powerful portrait of the first professional athlete, an all-pro football player, to discuss his homosexuality.

Richard Lapchick, **Five Minutes to Midnight**. The leading sports activist discusses sports and race in the '90s.

Peter Levine, **American Sport: A Documentary History**. A readable romp though primary sources with a leading sports historian.

John J. Macaloon, **This Great Symbol**. Baron Coubertin and the rise of the Olympic Games.

David Meggysey, **Out of Their League**. From stereotypical conservative jock to radical, a pro linebacker illuminates his politicization.

Mariah Burton Nelson, **Are We Winning Yet?** An anecdotal, contemporary account of the impact of women on sport, and vice-versa.

Benjamin G. Rader, **American Sports: From the Age of Folk Games to the Age of the Spectator**. This is considered the best over-all survey of the subject.

Lawrence Ritter, **The Glory of Their Times**. The classic oral history of the great old-time baseball players.

Jules Tygiel, **Baseball's Great Experiment**. An important and absorbing study of the causes and effects of Jackie Robinson's integration of the national pastime.

Babe Didrikson Zaharias, **This Life I've Led**. The other Babe, the greatest woman athlete of the century, Olympian, basketball player, golf champion, tells her story.

ROBERT LIPSYTE is a journalist and author. He is a sports columnist for *The New York Times* and previously reported for NBC and CBS News. His nonfiction books include *Assignment: Sports* and *SportsWorld: An American Dreamland*. His young adult novels include *The Contender, The Summerboy*, and *The Brave*.

DAVID PUTTNAM ON MOVIES

A Grammar of the Film by Raymond Spottiswode. First published in 1935, this remains for me a seminal work.

Picture by Lillian Ross. This classic account of the making of "The Red Badge of Courage" is still one of the finest portraits of a film in production.

Final Cut by Steven Bach. The classic contemporary equivalent to *Picture*. A wonderful account of the madness and mayhem behind the production of "Heaven's Gate" and a fascinating insight into the Hollywood of the late '70s.

Indecent Exposure by David McClintick. Another riveting account of contemporary Hollywood: McClintick's brilliant story of the Begelman scandal rocked the industry in the late '70s.

The Technique of Film Editing by Karel Reisz, 2nd edition. This remains one of the best insights into the art of film editing.

DAVID PUTTNAM is a movie producer whose films include "Chariots of Fire," "Local Hero," "The Killing Fields," and "The Mission." He was formerly chairman of Columbia Pictures.

M.F.K. FISHER ON FOOD

Larousse Gastronomique by Prosper Montagne. I prefer the French edition with the translation by Charlotte Turgeon. It is very good.

Mastering the Art of French Cooking (2 volumes) by Julia Child, Simone Beck, and Louise Berthold, revised edition. They are both considered very wordy, but if followed closely they are infallible. I use them for reference.

The Escoffier Cook Book by Auguste Escoffier. A good example of fancy hotel-type cooking, although it was thought to be very simple when it was written.

The New York Times Cookbook, revised edition. By far the best of any of the books edited by Craig Claiborne.

The Physiology of Taste by J.A. Brillat-Savarin. I use the

Fisher translation because it is by far the best, although it will be outdated soon.

M.F.K. FISHER was the author of more than 20 books on food. W.H. Auden once called her prose the best in America. Her first collection of essays, *Serve It Forth*, appeared in 1937. She is also the author of *How to Cook a Wolf* and *The Gastronomical Me*. She died in 1992.

ALICE WATERS ON FOOD

Elizabeth David's **French Country Cooking** and **Mediterranean Food**. For her wonderful food aesthetic.

Richard Olney, **The French Menu Cookbook**. For his focus on the seasonality of foods and for his taste in matching food and wines.

Waverly Root, **The Food of Italy** and **The Food of France**. Inspiring reference books.

M.F.K. Fisher, **Serve It Forth**. Sensuous food writing.

Diana Kennedy, **The Cuisine of Mexico**. Unusual, accurate, and delicious recipes.

Kaichi Tsuji, **Kaiseki Zen Tastes in Japanese Cooking**. Remarkable photographs and woodcuts.

Joy Larkcom, **The Salad Garden**. Wonderfully inspiring for the cook/gardener.

ALICE WATERS is a chef and restaurant owner. She opened Chez Panisse in Berkeley, California, in 1971, and her cooking has won several awards. Her books include *The Chez Panisse Menu Cookbook* and *Chez Panisse Cooking* (with Paul Bertolli).

GEORGE SHEEHAN ON FITNESS

The scientific definition of fitness is "the ability to do submaximal work to exhaustion." Fitness is, of course, much more than that. It is integral to health, which is described by the World Health Organization as "total physical, mental, and social well being."

Fitness adds hours to your day and years to your life. It increases your creative ability and your capacity to handle stress. Fitness also helps stabilize your emotional state. According to William James, it lends a background of sanity, serenity, and good humor to your life. It brings about a physiological and psychological transformation.

The principles and techniques that are fundamental to this metamorphosis can be found in books as far back as the ancient Greeks. For those interested in a reading list on the philosophy and techniques fundamental to a successful fitness program I would like to make a few suggestions.

First, however, I should say that fitness is such a basic quality that almost all of the important books recommended here will refer to it, if only indirectly. I can pick out almost any book on the shelves in front of me and find something relevant to fitness.

With that said, let me make a few recommendations, beginning with the philosophy of fitness.

Sport, a Philosophic Inquiry by Paul Weiss. Virtually the only full-dress consideration of sport by a philosopher. However, George Santayana's essay **Why I Sit in the Bleachers** and his consideration of sport in **The Last Puritan** summarize much that is valuable.

Talks to Teachers and **Essays of Faith and Morals** by William James. James was the philosopher of "The Experience." He was an Emersonian and had an enormous respect for the common man, the human body, and the world of sport.

Homo Ludens by Johan Huizinga. An investigation into the play element in our everyday life.

Sun and Steel by Yukio Mishima. The athletic experience described by a Nobel candidate for literature.

Meditations on Quixote by Ortega y Gasset. An exploration of the heroic in daily life which should lead you further into this philosopher of the common man.

To these I would add **Emerson, Thoreau, William Sheldon** and others who thought we must do our thing — but never presumed to tell us what our thing should be.

Next come suggestions of books that deal with the techniques. "Nature never overlooks a mistake or makes the slightest allowance for ignorance," wrote T.H. Huxley. Those rules are varied and many, but here we can confine them to three areas — exercise, diet, and stress management.

Fit for America: Health, Fitness, Sport and American Society by Harvey Green. An engrossing and instructive recounting of fitness movements in the United States since 1830. The theme is familiar: "The more things change, the more they remain the same."

The Paleolithic Prescription by S. Boyd Eaton, M.D., Marjorie Shostak, and Melvin Konner, M.D., Ph.D. A lifestyle derived from that of our "caveman" ancestors, this may be the program we were programmed for.

The Hibernation Response by Peter Whybrow, M.D. and Robert Bahr. An examination of the importance of our home and our diet to our well-being. A consideration of the contribution of sunlight, interior decorating, and differences in breakfast and supper to our quality of life.

Sports Nutrition Guidebook by Nancy Clark. America's leading sports nutritionist assures athletes of a long life as well as performance. Basic information on eating for health and energy.

The New Aerobics by Kenneth Cooper. The doctor and the system that set off the fitness boom in 1968.

The Complete Book of Running by Jim Fixx. The man and the information/motivation that sparked the running revolution.

The Care of the Self and **The Use of Pleasure** by Michel

Foucault. Masterly discussions of the classical Greeks' lifestyle. They will elevate your consciousness to the duties and obligations that accompany the good life.

Implicit in many of these books is stress management. In his essays William James has an excellent little essay on "The Gospel of Relaxation." The use of the word gospel is a happy one because it introduces the idea of religion which James called "the sovereign cure for anxiety."

Some practical, yet in a sense philosophical, texts I've found useful are:

Aequanimitas by William Osler. Advice from one of the great physicians.

How to Live on 24 Hours a Day by Arnold Bennett. This is a popular treatment of the Stoic philosophy found in Epictetus, Seneca, and Marcus Aurelius.

I would add one novel to this collection:

Report to Greco by Nikos Kazantzakis. A marvelous recounting of one person's total response of body, mind, and spirit to life.

The underlying theme of these books, stated or unstated, has to do with the creation of a self. "Life is a desperate struggle," wrote Ortega, "to become in fact what you are in design."

Fitness, which has to do with exercising all our faculties, is the way we achieve this goal. We are born with a 75-year warranty; it's time to read the instructions.

GEORGE SHEEHAN was a cardiologist and a lifelong runner. His many books include *Running and Being* and *Medical Advice for Runners*. He died in 1993.

HELEN SINGER KAPLAN ON SEX

Human Sexual Inadequacy by William Masters and Virginia Johnson.
For Yourself by Lonnie Barbach.
Male Sexuality by Bernie Zilbergeld.
My Secret Garden by Nancy Friday.
Love & Sex After 60 by Robert Butler.

HELEN SINGER KAPLAN is a psychiatrist and leading sex therapist. Her books include *The New Sex Therapy*, *Disorders of Sexual Desire*, *Making Sense of Sex*, and *Women and AIDS*.

FAYE WATTLETON ON SEX

My list focuses on family communications about sexuality.

The Family Book About Sexuality by Mary S. Calderone and Eric W. Johnson. Offers current information about numerous sexual issues in nontechnical and nonjudgmental language easily shared by parents and children.
Straight from the Heart: How to Talk to Your Teenager

About Love and Sex by Carol Cassell. A sexuality educator explains ways in which parents can broach difficult emotional and physiological issues relating to sexuality and love to their adolescent children.

A Parent's Guide to Teenage Sexuality by Jay Gale. Written by a psychologist, this guide helps parents communicate with their children about sexuality matters while focusing on teens' needs for self-esteem, self-expression, and understanding. It also addresses special situations such as sexual trauma, the single parent, and the handicapped teenager.

Raising a Child Conservatively in a Sexually Permissive World by Sol and Judith Gordon. Provides parents with middle-ground sound advice and good sense so that they can give their children a perspective on sex and sexuality somewhere between the freedom of the "sexual revolution" and unhealthy sexual censorship.

Getting Closer: Discover and Understand Your Child's Secret Feelings about Growing Up by Ellen Rosenberg. Provides suggestions for parents on how to talk about children's growth and sexual maturation, dating, social pressures, friendships and popularity, family relationships, separation, divorce and stepfamilies, death, disability, and prejudice.

Sex Is More Than a Plumbing Lesson: A Parents' Guide to Sexuality Education for Infants Through the Teen Years by Patty Stark. This readable guide presents sexuality in its broadest concept, in all the expressions of those things that make people unique. It empowers parents to communicate to their children, at every age level, personal values as well as sexual knowledge.

FAYE WATTLETON served as president of Planned Parenthood Federation of America from 1978 to 1991. She is the author, with Elisabeth Keiffer, of *How to Talk With Your Child About Sexuality: A Parent's Guide.*

REDMOND O'HANLON ON TRAVEL

The Malay Archipelago: The Land of the Orang-utan and the Bird of Paradise by Alfred Russel Wallace, 1869.
The Naturalist on the River Amazons by Henry Walter Bates, 1863.
Explorations and Adventures in Equatorial Africa by Paul B. Du Chaillu, 1861.
Dead Souls by Nikolai Gogol, 1842.
The Adventures of Don Quixote by Miguel de Cervantes, 1615.

REDMOND O'HANLON is a writer. His books include *Into the Heart of Borneo* and *In Trouble Again: A Journey Between the Orinoco and the Amazon.*

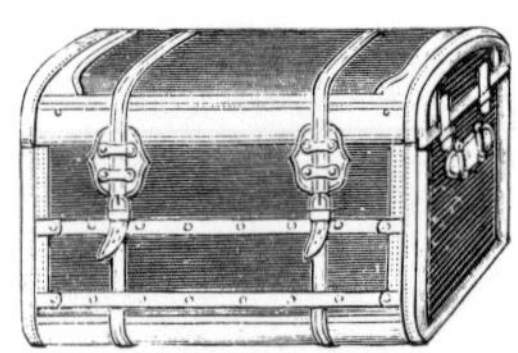

ERIC BOGOSIAN ON AMERICAN HUMOR

The goal of comedy is laughs. On the other hand, humor must have an aftereffect to be truly great. Humor, which focuses on the way we are as human beings, needs meat on its bones. Topical political satire, for instance, is not humor. And yet there are many gray areas, as in the work of Richard Pryor or W.C. Fields.

In the realm of American literature (as opposed to what you can listen to on record or video), I dig the sardonic. Head and shoulders above all is Mark Twain, the greatest. Read **Letters from the Earth** or anything else. More recently, **James Thurber**'s collections of short stories are deceptively sweet.

Lenny Bruce left us **How to Talk Dirty and Influence People**. And if you really want to get nasty, Stephen King's short stories are happy to take you over the edge. Finally, the grimmest stuff is somehow the funniest, check out **Harry Crews' Body**.

ERIC BOGOSIAN is a performer and writer who starred in his play and movie "Talk Radio." His solo performance works include "Drinking in America," "FunHouse," and "Sex, Drugs, Rock 'n Roll," all of which have appeared in book form as well. He also wrote *Notes from Underground.*

ERMA BOMBECK

The title that always comes to the top for me is Anne Morrow Lindbergh's **Gift from the Sea**. Take away the most visible human being on the planet as a husband and our lives were in some ways parallel. We were trying to balance children, family, and a sense of self. In her quiet, dignified way she was the forerunner of the women's movement.

All of **Robert Benchley**'s books had an impact on me because I wanted to grow a mustache and be just like him. To me he epitomized the best of humor. It was self-effacing, gentle, didn't hurt anyone, and made me laugh uproariously. After all these years, I can still recall passages from his wonderful books. Take your pick of any one of them and it's my favorite.

William Manchester has an impact on my life because, after reading him, I wanted to quit writing forever and declare myself totally inadequate. The man had such a way with words and was so gifted, I paled, as most of us did.

Maybe because I was in my teenage years, but **Max Shulman** really affected my decision for a career in humor. I couldn't imagine how someone could take a simple fact, exaggerate it to the point of absurdity, put it on a blank piece of paper, and make people forget all their problems. When I read about his exploits at the University of Minnesota, I knew I wanted to do that.

ERMA BOMBECK has been a syndicated columnist since 1965 and her column currently appears in over 900 newspapers. Her books include *The Grass is Always Greener Over the Septic Tank*; *If Life is a Bowl of Cherries, What Am I Doing in the Pits?*; and *When You Look Like Your Passport Photo, It's Time to Go Home*.

CHAPTER 6
SCIENCE AND NATURE

Due to our living in the information age, there has been a remarkable popularization of science; witness Stephen Hawking's seemingly endless tenure on the bestseller lists with *A Brief History of Time.* But there has long existed a body of enduring classics — *The Closing Circle* and *Silent Spring*, *On the Origin of Species*, and *Walden*, for example — formed from the discoveries, insights, and future warnings of scientists and naturalists and those who write about them. In their attempts to tackle vital issues such as solving world hunger or hunting down the quark, scientists have not only shared their knowledge but have also invited readers to participate in shaping Earth's future and understanding its past. Such a partnership will only be strengthened by the smart, compelling reading lists found in this chapter.

CARL DJERASSI ON SCIENCE

James D. Watson, **The Double Helix**. A brutally honest personal view of one of the most important discoveries in 20th century biology.

Anne Sayre, **Rosalind Franklin and DNA**. A woman's view

of the same events recorded by Watson.

Erwin Chargaff, **Heraclitean Fire: Sketches From a Life Before Nature**. One of the most literate scientific autobiographies of the last two decades.

Londa Schiebinger, **The Mind Has No Sex?** A first-class commentary on the origins of women's contributions to modern science.

Aldous Huxley, **Brave New World** and **Brave New World Revisited**. Futuristic classics that still merit reading, preferably in conjunction with Szilard's short stories.

Leo Szilard, **The Voice of the Dolphin and Other Stories**. These futuristic stories by one of the most brilliant physicists of the atomic age are startlingly prescient.

Lewis Thomas, **The Lives of a Cell** and **The Medusa and the Snail**. Among the most elegant and readable essays on biomedical topics written by a scientist.

CARL DJERASSI is a writer and a professor of chemistry at Stanford University. He received the National Medal of Science for developing the first steroid oral contraceptive. His books include *The Politics of Contraception: Birth Control in the Year 2001*; *Cantor's Dilemma*, a novel; and *The Pill, Pygmy Chimps, and Degas's Horse: An Autobiography.*

FREEMAN DYSON ON SCIENCE

For the general reader interested in science, here are three books in each of four categories: literary, biographical, futuristic, and expository.

Literary:

Voyages to the Moon by Marjorie Hope Nicholson. The literary background of the exploration of space.

The World, the Flesh and the Devil by J.D. Bernal, originally published in 1929. Bernal called this "An enquiry into the future of the three enemies of the rational soul."

Geometry and the Liberal Arts by Dan Pedoe. Dan Pedoe taught me in high school 50 years ago and infected me with his passion for geometry.

Biographical:

The Religion of Isaac Newton by Frank Manuel. Going back to the original unpublished manuscripts in Jerusalem, Manuel finds a Newton very different from the public figure he later became.

Discovery, Invention, Research by Fritz Zwicky. Autobiography of a cantankerous genius who was also a great astronomer.

What Do You Care What Other People Think? by Richard Feynman and Ralph Leighton. Anecdotal history of another cantankerous genius, the physicist Richard Feynman.

Futuristic:

Spaceships of the Mind by Nigel Calder. Script of a BBC television series on space exploration regarded as an expression of human culture.

2081, A Hopeful View of the Human Future by Gerard K. O'Neill. A voice dissenting from the fashionable prophets of doom and gloom.

Engines of Creation by K. Eric Drexler. Drexler believes that the big changes in human society will come from the technology of tiny machines operating on a microscopic scale.

Expository:

The Free Three Minutes by Steve Weinberg. A short and lucid account of what we know about the early universe and how we know it.

The New Physics, edited by Paul Davis. An anthology of expository articles by leading astronomers and physicists, for serious students only.

The World Treasury of Physics, Astronomy and Mathematics, edited by Timothy Ferris. A much less technical anthology, going back into history and including some poetry.

FREEMAN DYSON has been professor of physics at the Institute for Advanced Study since 1953. His work has received several awards, including the Max Planck Medal and the J. Robert Oppenheimer Memorial Prize. His books include *Disturbing the Universe* and *Origins of Life*.

Nature and Nature's laws lay hid in night:
God said, Let Newton be! and all was light!
— Alexander Pope

ROBERT HAZEN ON SCIENCE

I've selected a baker's dozen of my favorite popular science titles, representing a wide range of science topics and writing styles, but all written to be enjoyed by nonscientists. I have neglected several wonderful books on medical science by Jonathan Miller, Oliver Sacks, and Lewis Thomas, among others. Also missing from my list are the best popular books on technology, such as Tracy Kidder's *The Soul of a New Machine*, David Macaulay's *How Things Work*, and Tom Wolfe's *The Right Stuff*. But here are my picks for physics, chemistry, geology, and biology.

On the Origin of Species: A Facsimile of the First Edition by Charles Darwin, originally published in 1859. Although this book changed the western world and is still the focus of acrimonious debate, few have read the original. You might be surprised at how meticulous, cautious, and understated Darwin was in presenting his revolutionary thesis.

God and the New Physics by Paul Davies. Davies's popular books on physics and cosmology place him among the best modern science writers. He is a distinguished theoretical physicist who knows how to translate the complexities of relativity, quantum mechanics, and other nonintuitive science concepts into elegant English prose.

Coming of Age in the Milky Way by Timothy Ferris. There are a dozen popular books about the origins and present state of the universe, but I think this is the most sweeping and successful. Science, history, and philosophy are combined to explain how "our species has arrived at its current estimation of the dimensions of cosmic space and time."

Chaos by James Gleick. In spite of an occasionally intrusive journalistic style, Gleick manages to capture the excitement and dynamics of the fast-growing field of nonpredictable (chaotic) physical systems. Many other popular texts on chaos have followed, but this is still the classic.

Cartoon Guide to Genetics by Larry Gonick and Mark Wheelis. This book has to be the best popular overview of genetics — the centerpiece of modern biology — in the history of the universe. A difficult subject is made easy and funny at the same time. I can't wait to read Gonick's *Cartoon Guide to Physics.*

The New Science of Strong Materials: Or Why You Don't Fall Through the Floor by J.E. Gordon. A wonderful introduction to the chemistry and physics of everyday materials. Gordon shows how the properties of everyday materials, from plywood to reinforced concrete, arise from their distinctive atomic arrangements.

Bully for Brontosaurus and **The Panda's Thumb** by Stephen Jay Gould. Gould, perhaps the finest science writer of our time, periodically assembles essays from his *This View* *of Life* column in *Natural History* magazine. Gould has an amazing gift for seeing the big picture in nature's minutiae.

Great Scientific Experiments by Rom Harre. This intimate look at 20 seminal experiments explains the why and how of scientific research. The investigations described span centuries, but reveal a unity in the quest for scientific knowledge.

Rising from the Plains by John McPhee. McPhee shares the poetry of geology in his epic tales of the earth's past and present.

The Hunting of the Quark by Michael Riordan. Particle physics is one of the most abstract scientific fields, yet physicist Riordan succeeds in interweaving his science with an exciting narrative of discovery. As good an inside account of science and scientists as you're likely to read.

Landprints: On the Magnificent American Landscape by Walter Sullivan. This is my favorite of several fine books by Sullivan, former science editor of *The New York Times* and dean of American science journalists. *Landprints* features dozens of superb aerial photographs of the American countryside, with lucid explanations of the underlying geology and biology. A must-read for any frequent flyer.

Meditations at 10,000 Feet by James Trefil. Perhaps the best of Trefil's excellent series of books on our world. He combines his keen scientific insight with a reverence for his favorite Montana haunts. You'll discover fascinating stories about phenomena from plate tectonics to twisted trees.

The Double Helix by James Watson. Nobel Prize-winner Watson provides a short, incisive, and often controversial first-hand account of one of the great scientific discoveries of our time. Historians may argue with some of his interpretations of events, particularly the key work of Rosalind Franklin, but this book remains one of the best inside accounts of intense, competitive research.

ROBERT M. HAZEN is a research scientist at the Carnegie Institute of Washington's Geophysical Laboratory and is the Robinson Professor of Earth Science at George Mason University. Besides his scholarly research, Hazen, along with James Trefil, has worked to present scientific ideas to the general public. They are the authors of *Science Matters: Achieving Scientific Literacy.*

GERARD PIEL ON SCIENCE

How do we know what we know? That is the first thing all of us who are not scientists need to understand about science. From this we can gain humility and confidence in what we think we understand about anything.

In **Science and Common Sense**, James Bryant Conant shows how by common sense, which the scientist learns, by practice, to practice with some rigor, we get to know something with reasonable but never absolute certainty. From Percy W. Bridgman, in **Reflections of a Physicist**, we learn this task is "as private as my toothache."

In **The Sociology of Science**, Robert K. Merton demonstrates the public nature of this private enterprise: how we can know because we can trust someone else's knowing.

The next thing we need to know about science is how this private-public enterprise has changed and goes on changing the human condition — in the words of Alfred North Whitehead, "The essence of freedom is the practicability of purpose...Prometheus did not bring to mankind freedom of the press. He procured fire."

Read **Adventures of Ideas** by Whitehead; **Nine Chains to the Moon** by R. Buckminster Fuller; **Enough and to Spare** by Kirtley Mather; **On Living in a Revolution** by Julian Huxley; and every year, the **Human Development Report** from the United Nations Development Program.

P.S.: You don't need to know the names of the amino acids, the difference between schist and gneiss, the interior temperature of the Sun, the atomic weight of U235, the wavelength of UV radiation — unless you would like to!

GERARD PIEL is the founder, former publisher, and chairman emeritus of *Scientific American* magazine. His books include *Science in the Cause of Man*; *The Acceleration of History*; and *Only One World, Our Own to Make and to Keep.*

Familiar things happen, and mankind does not
bother about them. It requires a very unusual mind
to undertake the analysis of the obvious.
— Alfred North Whitehead, *Science and the Modern World*

WENDELL BERRY ON FARMING

F.H. King, **Farmers of Forty Centuries**
Joseph Russell Smith, **Tree Crops**
Sir Albert Howard, **The Soil and Health** and **An Agricultural Testament**
Wes Jackson, **New Roots for Agriculture** and **Altars of Unhewn Stone**
Wes Jackson, Wendell Berry, and Bruce Colman, editors, **Meeting the Expectations of the Land**
Judy Soule and Jon Piper, **Farming in Nature's Image: An Ecological Approach to Agriculture**

WENDELL BERRY is a novelist, poet, teacher, and farmer. His novels include *A Place on Earth* and *The Memory of Old Jack*. His other books include *Collected Poems, 1957-1982*; *What Are People For?: Essays*; and *Fidelity: Five Stories*.

EARL BUTZ ON FARMING

The Farm Fiasco by James Bovard. This is a provocative book by America's leading critic of federal policy. It is hard-hitting, effectively written, and well documented.

Trees, Why Do You Wait?: America's Changing Rural Culture by Richard Critchfield. Critchfield writes knowingly of two rural communities, one in North Dakota and one in Iowa. He sees these rural communities as threatened by urbanization, with the consequent erosion of traditional values and the work ethic.

Ending Hunger: An Idea Whose Time Has Come by the Hunger Project. This is a huge book, well-supplied with charts, tables, and color pictures; written in lucid form; factually reliable; guardedly optimistic about world food prospects, as the title indicates.

Toward a Well-Fed World by Don Paarlberg. This book traces the conquest of hunger from the earliest times. The overcoming of hunger is seen as proceeding on three fronts: agricultural science, food aid, and family planning. The contributions of 30 different hunger fighters are reported.

Agriculture and the Environment, edited by Tim T. Phipps, Pierre R. Crosson, and Kent A. Price. This is a balanced view of the current agricultural issues regarding the environment, written in understandable fashion by 20 well-qualified writers. Erosion, water quality, pesticides, and wetlands issues are addressed.

Farm: A Year in the Life of an American Farmer by

Richard Rhodes. This is a well-written, technically accurate story of a year's experience on a Missouri farm, written by the author of the 1988 Pulitzer Prize-winning history, *The Making of the Atomic Bomb*.

EARL L. BUTZ is Dean Emeritus of Agriculture at Purdue University. Butz served as Assistant Secretary of Agriculture under President Eisenhower and as Secretary of Agriculture under President Nixon.

KATHLEEN COURRIER ON THE ENVIRONMENT

Ten classic environmental books (in chronological order):

Silent Spring by Rachel Carson. *Silent Spring* is to the beginnings of environmental awareness what Harriet Beecher Stowe's *Uncle Tom's Cabin* was to the end of slavery. This expose of the "biocidal" effects of pesticides in general and DDT in particular is credited with getting DDT off the market in the United States, drumming up support for the creation of the Environmental Protection Agency, and opening the way for women in environmental science. Indeed, Carson is remembered above all as a committed scientist with the courage to challenge conventional wisdom.

The Closing Circle by Barry Commoner. Warning that "any living thing that hopes to live on the earth must fit into the ecosphere or perish," Commoner's enduring insight is that the absolute amount of industrial production isn't the sole or even main determinant of pollution. Rather, it's what we produce and how. In *The Closing Circle*, he familiarized millions of Americans with the basic principles of ecology — most notably, that there is no free lunch and that in the natural world everything is connected to everything else.

The Limits to Growth by Donella Meadows, et al. With worldwide sales of four million copies, this book stirred up a tempest over whether a growing population would soon exhaust such resources as fossil fuels, food, and minerals. In the cool language of science, Meadows and the book's other authors predicted the crash of population and industry within a century if various trends then in force didn't change. This pathbreaking book had many critics, but it legitimated the use of computer models to predict possible environmental futures.

Only One Earth by Barbara Ward and René Dubos. Ward and Dubos were among the first to look to both science and the wisdom of the ancients for ways to keep the downside of economic growth — environmental degradation and the growing gulf between rich and poor — within bounds. The authors were ahead of their time (and ours), voicing concern about the greenhouse effect, fossil fuel dependence, Los Angeles-style congestion, and recognizing the need to rethink self-interest and national interests in view of escalating demands on Earth's resources.

Small Is Beautiful: Economics as if People Mattered by E.F. Schumacher. With this book, E.F. Schumacher founded "Buddhist economics" (the notion that local communities can become nearly self-sufficient using natural resources sparingly) and the "appropriate technology" movement (the attempt to avoid the debt, high unemployment, and environmental costs of most large-scale technologies by switching to smaller-scale decentralized technologies). An admirer of Gandhi, Schumacher gave credence in the West to the belief that technology should be harnessed first and foremost to alleviate poverty, and that virtue and values must figure centrally in technology choice.

Soft Energy Paths: Toward a Durable Peace by Amory B. Lovins. Physicist and gadfly Amory Lovins pointed out 15 years ago that utility executives and energy policy-makers have been on the wrong track. The first question to ask isn't, "Where do we get the energy we need?" It is, "What do we need energy for?" Matching energy needs to energy sources, Lovins made a still-compelling case for saving money and the environment by employing conservation and a broad range of technologies and renewable energy sources — wind, hydropower, direct sunlight, etc. His underlying message? Oil spills, nuclear accidents, and Mid-East involvement are *not* part of the price we have to pay for energy.

Man and the Natural World: A History of the Modern Sensibility by Keith Thomas. To Thomas goes credit for tracing through history the slow but steady evolution of the idea that human beings have an obligation to the rest of creation. His tour of religion, science, and culture shows brilliantly how people slowly endowed "beasts" and landscapes with souls and rights and recently came to wonder if perhaps doing so doesn't serve humankind better than enslaving nature does. Thomas makes readers realize that the environmental movement was centuries in the making.

Biophilia: The Human Bond with Other Species by E.O. Wilson. A man in love with his work makes for good reading, and if his work is saving the world's species, so much the better for the reader and the world. *Biophilia* beautifully captures both the excitement and the drudgery of scientific exploration and imparts a keen sense of the importance of species – whether known to science or not – to the web of life. In a typically lyrical passage, Pulitzer Prize-winner Wilson writes that cutting down a rainforest to make way for economic development is like "burning a Renaissance painting to cook dinner." Few books have been quoted as often by scientists and environmental writers as this one.

Home Economics by Wendell Berry. With soil, trees, minerals, and the rest of the "stuff of creation" dirt cheap compared to labor, time, and money, it's no wonder, says Berry, that people chew up the environment (and other people) in the name of sound economic practice. Berry's great contribution is showing how finding humankind's right relation to the natural world requires making a commitment to the local environment and forsaking no-holds-barred individualism for communitarian value.

Our Common Future by the World Commission on Environment and Development. This United Nations-sponsored report on the well-being of the planet and its inhabitants picks up where *Only One Earth* left off. Calling for economic development that "meets the needs of the present without compromising the ability of future generations to meet their own needs," this book sets a politically realistic agenda based on global justice. Outside of the United States, it has prompted national action and a spirited public debate.

KATHLEEN COURRIER directs the publishing program at the World Resources Institute in Washington, D.C., which is best known for its annual *State of the World Report*. She has written for *Sierra*, *The Washington Post*, *The Christian Science Monitor*, and *Technology Review*.

The great majority of economists are still pursuing
the absurd ideal of making their "science" as scientific and
precise as physics; as if there were no qualitative
differences between mindless atoms and men
made in the image of God.
— E.F. Schumacher, *Small Is Beautiful*

DAVE FOREMAN ON CONSERVATION

I recommend a basic six-pack of books for conservationists. They are:

A Sand County Almanac by Aldo Leopold. This is the most important, the loveliest, and wisest book ever penned. All modern conservation activism and philosophy begins with this book.

Overshoot by William R. Catton. Sociology professor Catton applies the ecological concept of carrying capacity to human beings and shows that we have already "overshot" the carrying capacity of Earth.

The Arrogance of Humanism by David Ehrenfeld. Ehrenfeld, editor of the *Journal of Conservation Biology*, demolishes anthropocentric arrogance and argues lovingly and forcefully for a biocentric world view, ethic, and conservation strategy.

Desert Solitaire by Edward Abbey. This is the book that launched me and thousands of others onto the wilderness conservation trail. Unlike much "nature writing," it's full of piss and vinegar.

Wilderness and the American Mind by Roderick Nash. This peerless history of American attitudes toward the wilderness is the most important book available for understanding the dynamic interplay between humans and nature in the New World.

Wilderness on the Rocks by Howie Wolke. Conservationist and professional wilderness guide Wolke critiques establishment conservation and calls for a true conservation based on biological diversity instead of "rocks and ice" scenery and recreation.

DAVE FOREMAN is chairman of The Wildlands Project and executive editor of *Wild Earth* magazine. He was formerly Southwest Representative for the Wilderness Society and co-founder of Earth First! His books include *Confessions of an Eco-Warrior* and *The Big Outside*, written with Howie Wolke.

GILBERT GROSVENOR ON GEOGRAPHY

All Possible Worlds: A History of Geographical Ideas by Preston E. James and Geoffrey J. Martin, 2nd edition. Considers the entire field of geography from its early classical beginnings in the Mediterranean world to the contemporary period with its new methods of observation and analysis. A highly readable treatise on the history of geographic thought.

Closeup: How to Read a City by Grady Clay. Pioneering effort that shows the reader how to understand the past and present, and predict the future of cities by interpreting the visible clues on the urban landscape.

Exploring Your World: The Adventure of Geography, edited by Donald Crump. Begins with a discourse on "What is Geography" and continues with encyclopedic discussions and examples of more than 300 geographic terms. Lavishly illustrated and captioned.

The Geographer's Art by Peter Haggett. A view of geography by a world-renowned geographer who explains why he finds the subject so fascinating. Considers geography's spatial approach in interpreting and understanding patterns, structure, and processes that give meaning to the world's regional diversity.

Geography's Inner Worlds: Pervasive Themes in Contemporary American Geography, edited by Ronald F. Abler, Melvin G. Marcus, and Judy M. Olson. Explores core ideas and themes in geography.

The Geographer at Work by Peter Gould. A well-known geographer writes about the contemporary world of geography with a focus on the utility of using the geographic approach and the new technologies such as computers and satellites in such areas as transportation, medicine, agricultural development, and communications.

Geography: Regions and Concepts by H.J. DeBlij and Peter O. Muller, 6th edition. Introductory college text with comprehensive coverage of world regions. Each chapter includes a systematic essay on a variety of subjects including population geography, climatology, historical geography, economic geography, and cultural geography.

The Human Mosaic: A Thematic Introduction to Cultural Geography by Terry G. Jordan and Lester Rowntree, 4th edition. An introductory text that looks at the spatial imprint of humans on the landscape through the themes of population, agriculture, politics, languages, folk and popular culture, and others.

The Nine Nations of North America by Joel Garreau. By a journalist, this is a good use of regional analysis in geography for the general population. Considers a thought-provoking regionalization of the United States including New England, the Foundry, Dixie, the Islands, Mexamerica, Ectopia, the Empty Quarter, the Breadbasket, and Quebec.

Physical Geography: A Landscape Appreciation by Tom McKnight. Introductory college-level textbook which encourages an understanding and appreciation of everything outside the window that stimulates our senses. Excellent examples supplement the text.

GILBERT GROSVENOR is president and chairman of The National Geographic Society.

DENIS HAYES ON THE ENVIRONMENT

Silent Spring by Rachel Carson. Showed that the adverse effects of industrial chemistry can be widespread, long-lived, and have dire unanticipated consequences. It also demonstrated the leaden mantra of vested interests.

The Population Bomb by Paul Ehrlich. Brought Malthus up to date and made him readable.

The Curve of Binding Energy by John McPhee. McPhee makes the complex interrelationship between nuclear power and weapons proliferation understandable through this impressive biography of Ted Taylor.

Desert Solitaire by Edward Abbey. Abbey can move even those who have never experienced the wild, or felt true aloneness, or seen up close the fire in a wolf's eyes.

The End of Nature by Bill McKibben. Addresses the major global environmental issues with poetic honesty.

A book that had a certain impact on me personally was Joseph Heller's **Catch 22**. I carried this book in my packsack for three years as I hitch-hiked through 60+ countries. For me, the act of growing up required that I confront Heller's absurdities and push beyond them to find some meaning in life. Funny as hell and deeply moving.

DENIS HAYES helped to found Earth Day in 1970, and was director of the national Solar Energy Research Institute from 1979 to 1981. He is author of *Rays of Hope* and is a lawyer in San Francisco.

HAZEL HENDERSON ON THE ENVIRONMENT

These books all gave me a sense of where I was in time and space as well as what the important issues were at this stage of our human journey on this miraculous planet.

Spaceship Earth by Barbara Ward.
Small Is Beautiful by E.F. Schumacher.
The Underside of History by Elise Boulding.
The Myth of the Machine by Lewis Mumford.
Propaganda by Jacques Ellul.
The Entropy Law and the Economic Process by Nicholas Georgescu-Roegen. (He is the only economist worth studying, except for his student, Herman Daly.)
The Politics of Women's Spirituality by Charlene Spretnak.
The Possible Human by Jean Houston.
The Self-Organizing Universe by Erich Jantsch.
Gaia: The Human Journey from Chaos to Cosmos by Elisabet Sahtouris.
Structural Stability and Morphogenesis by Rene Thom.
The Tao of Physics by Fritjof Capra.
Mind and Nature by Gregory Bateson.
The Chalice and the Blade by Riane Eisler.
Androgyny by June Singer.
Pure Lust by Mary Daly.
The Reflexive Universe by Arthur Young.
The Future of Muslim Civilization by Ziauddin Sardar.
The Evolutionary Journey by Barbara Marx Hubbard.

HAZEL HENDERSON is a futurist and consultant on alternative paths for human development. Her books include *Creating Alternative Futures*, *The Politics of the Solar Age*, and *Paradigms in Progress: Life Beyond Economics.*

AARON BECK ON PSYCHOLOGY

Albert Bandura, **Social Learning Theory**
Albert Ellis, **Reason and Emotion in Psychotherapy**
George Kelly, **The Psychology of Personal Constructs**
Michael J. Mahoney, **Cognition and Behavior Modification**
Donald H. Meichenbaum, **Cognitive Behavior Modification: An Integrative Approach**
H. Spielberg, **The Phenomenological Movement** (2 volumes)

DR. AARON BECK is a professor of psychiatry at the University of Pennsylvania and chief of the psychiatry department at Philadelphia General Hospital. His books include *Diagnosis and Management of Depression*; *Cognitive Therapy and the Emotional Disorders*; and *Anxiety and Phobias: Cognitive Approaches.*

MICHAEL E. DEBAKEY ON MEDICINE AND HEALTH

Medicine: Preserving the Passion by Phil Manning and Lois DeBakey.

The Heart, Arteries and Veins, edited by Willis Hurst, et al.

Textbook of Surgery: The Biological Basis of Modern Surgical Practice, 14th edition, edited by David Sabiston, Jr.

DR. MICHAEL E. DEBAKEY is a heart surgeon and medical inventor and innovator. He has performed more than 50,000 cardiovascular procedures and has trained more than 1,000 surgeons. He has been affiliated with the Baylor College of Medicine in Houston, where he is now chancellor, since 1948. He is also director of the school's DeBakey Heart Center. He is the author of *The Living Heart*, with Antonio Gotto, and *The Living Heart Diet* with Antonio Gotto, Lynne Scott, and John Foreyt.

DANIEL J. KEVLES ON GENETICS

François Jacob, **The Logic of Life: A History of Heredity** (translated by Betty E. Spillman). An elegant rendering of ideas of heredity from the earliest biochemical views of life through molecular genetics.

Horace Freeland Judson, **The Eighth Day of Creation: Makers of the Revolution in Biology**. A magisterial account of the development of the molecular biology of the gene.

Melvin Konner, **The Tangled Wing: Biological Constraints on the Human Spirit**. A compellingly written treatment, at once scientifically restrained and insightful, about the role that genes may play in the evolution of human behavior.

Robert Proctor, **Racial Hygiene: Medicine Under the Nazis**. A graphic inquiry into how distortions of genetics were used for barbarous purposes and, by implication, a cautionary instruction for our own day.

A. H. Sturtevant, **A History of Genetics**. A useful overview by one of the principal scientists in the development of classical genetics.

DANIEL J. KEVLES is the Keopfli Professor of Humanities at the California Institute of Technology. His books include *In The Name of Eugenics: Genetics and the Uses of Human Heredity*; *The Physicists: The History of a Scientific Community in Modern America*; and *The Code of Codes: Scientific and Social Issues in the Human Genome Project*.

RUTH MACKLIN ON BIOETHICS

George J. Annas, **Judging Medicine** and **The Rights of Patients**, 2nd edition

Tom L. Beauchamp and James Childress, **Principles of**

Biomedical Ethics, 3rd edition
Tom L. Beauchamp and Ruth Faden, **A History and Theory of Informed Consent**
Norman Daniels, **Just Health Care**
Samuel Gorovitz, **Doctors' Dilemma: Moral Conflict and Medical Care**
James Rachels, **The End of Life: Euthanasia and Morality**
Peter Singer and Deanne Wells, **The Reproduction Revolution: New Ways of Making Babies**
Robert Veatch, **A Theory of Medical Ethics**

RUTH MACKLIN is a professor of bioethics at the Albert Einstein College of Medicine in Bronx, New York. She is the author of *Mortal Choices: Ethical Dilemmas in Modern Medicine* and *Man, Mind, and Morality: The Ethics of Behavior Control.*

JAKE PAGE ON ANIMALS

The Origin of Species by Charles Darwin. Very simply, the framework without which there can be no understanding of animals.

Evolution of the Vertebrates by Edwin H. Colbert. A superb review by the grand old man of the field.

Wonderful Life by Stephen Jay Gould. A wonderful account of some bizarre events in the Pre-Cambrian seas (and of how biologists think).

The Forest and the Sea by Marston Bates. A classically readable introduction to the creatures of two ecosystems.

Of Wolves and Men by Barry Lopez. A brilliant account of the lives of wolves and their reputation at the hands of man.

The Ecological Theater and The Evolutionary Play by G. Evelyn Hurchinson. Elegant essays by the late master of ecological thinking.

Sociobiology by Edward O. Wilson. A controversial modern attempt to encompass the nature of all life.

Biophilia by Edward O. Wilson. A wise exploration of the human bond with other species.

The Bird of Light by John Hay. Quite possibly the most beautiful book ever written about an animal — in this case, terns.

Through a Window by Jane Goodall. An astounding picture of our nearest relative, the chimpanzee, by the woman who has revolutionized our way of making such approaches.

JAKE PAGE, former editor of *Natural History* and *Smithsonian* magazines, is the author of 15 books, including *Zoo: The Modern Ark*; *Lords of the Air: The Smithsonian Book of Birds*; and *Animal Talk: Science and the Voices of Nature.*

GEORGE B. SCHALLER ON ANIMALS AND NATURE

Classic travel accounts by biologists:

Charles Darwin, 1839, **Voyage of H.M.S. Beagle**
Henry Bates, 1863, **The Naturalist on the River Amazons**
Alfred Wallace, 1868, **The Malay Archipelago**

Evocative books of naturalists afield:

William Beebe, 1920, **Jungle Peace**
Barry Lopez, 1986, **Arctic Dreams**
Archie Carr, 1964, **Ulendo: Travels of a Naturalist in Africa**
Archie Carr, 1956, **The Windward Road**
Edward Abbey, 1968, **Desert Solitaire**
Joseph Wood Krutch, 1952, **The Desert Year**
John Muir, 1894, **The Mountains of California**
Konrad Lorenz, 1952, **King Solomon's Ring**
Theodora Stanwell-Fletcher, 1946, **Driftwood Valley**
Henry David Thoreau, 1854, **Walden**
Annie Dillard, 1974, **Pilgrim at Tinker Creek**
Edward Hoagland, 1976, **Red Wolves and Black Bears**
Peter Matthiessen, 1972, **The Tree Where Man Was Born**
Sigurd Olson, 1956, **The Singing Wilderness**
Niko Tinbergen, 1958, **Curious Naturalists**
Margaret Murie, 1962, **Two in the Far North**

General books on nature:

Loren Eiseley, 1956, **The Immense Journey**
Edward Wilson, 1978, **On Human Nature**
René Dubos, 1972, **A God Within**
Rachel Carson, 1962, **Silent Spring**
Aldo Leopold, 1949, **Sand County Almanac**
Donald Griffin, 1984, **Animal Thinking**

Accounts of species:

Barry Lopez, 1978, **Of Wolves and Men**
Jane Goodall, 1971, **In the Shadow of Man**
Gavin Maxwell, 1960, **Ring of Bright Water**
Cynthia Moss, 1988, **Elephant Memories**
Joy Adamson, 1960, **Born Free**
George Schaller, 1963, **The Year of the Gorilla**

Scientific books:

Edward R. Wilson, 1975, **Sociobiology**
B. Smuts et al. (editors), 1987, **Primate Societies**
Karl Von Frisch, 1950, **Bees: Their Vision, Chemical Senses and Language**
J. Chapman and G. Feldhamer (editors), 1982, **Wild Mammals of North America**

GEORGE B. SCHALLER is director of the international wildlife conservation program of the New York Zoological Society. His field trips have taken him to Tanzania, Nepal, and China. His books include *The Year of the Gorilla*, *The Serengeti Lion*, and *Mountain Monarchs: Wild Sheep and Goats of the Himalayas.*

ANDREW WEIL ON MEDICINE AND HEALTH

The Body Electric: Electromagnetism and the Foundation of Life by Robert O. Becker and Gary Selden.
Diet for a New America by John Robbins.
Dr. Dean Ornish's Program for Reversing Heart Disease by Dean Ornish.

DR. ANDREW WEIL teaches at the College of Medicine at the University of Arizona and also has a general medical practice in Tucson. His books include *The Natural Mind*; *Health and Healing*; and *Natural Health, Natural Medicine: A Comprehensive Manual for Wellness and Self Care.*

JOHN ALLEN PAULOS ON MATHEMATICS

The following books are accessible to the general reader. They contain few equations and emphasize mathematical ideas, not routine computations or rigorous proofs. The list is a random sampler and makes absolutely no pretensions to completeness, uniform coverage of disciplines, or any other desiderata. It is simply a place to start: some good books selected from a much larger set, many members of which could, with equal justification, have been influential.

Edwin A. Abbot, **Flatland**
Donald J. Albers and G.L. Alexanderson, editors, **Mathematical People**
Petr Beckmann, **A History of Pi**
Eric Temple Bell, **Mathematics: Queen and Servant of Science**
Carl Boyer, **A History of Mathematics**
COMAP: (Consortium for Mathematics and its Applications),**For All Practical Purposes: Introduction to Contemporary Mathematics**
Richard Courant and Herbert Robbins, **What Is Mathematics?**
Philip Davis and Reuben Hersh, **The Mathematical Experience**
Martin Gardner, **Aha! Insight** and **Aha! Gotcha**
James Gleick, **Chaos: Making a New Science**
G.H. Hardy, **A Mathematician's Apology**
Douglas Hofstadter, **Godel, Escher, and Bach**
Georges Ifrah, **From One to Zero: A Universal History of Numbers**
Morris Kline, **Mathematics: An Introduction to Its Spirit and Use**
J.E. Littlewood, edited by Bollobas Bela, **Littlewood's Miscellany**
Benoit Mandelbrot, **The Fractal Geometry of Nature**
David S. Moore, **Statistics: Concepts and Controversies**
Edward Packel, **The Mathematics of Games and Gambling**
Theoni Pappas, **The Joy of Mathematics**
George Polya, **How to Solve It**
Ivars Peterson, **The Mathematical Tourist**

Rudy Rucker, **Mind Tools**
Warren Weaver, **Lady Luck**

JOHN ALLEN PAULOS is a professor of mathematics at Temple University in Philadelphia. His books include *Innumeracy: Mathematical Illiteracy and Its Consequences* and *Beyond Numeracy: Ruminations of a Numbers Man.*

CHEN NING YANG ON PHYSICS

Ideas and Opinions by Albert Einstein. A collection of Einstein's articles addressed to the layman, covering such topics as society, education, and Middle East disputes, and includes popular articles about physics as well.

CHEN NING YANG is a Nobel Prize-winner in physics who teaches at the State University of New York at Stony Brook. He is the author of *Elementary Particles: A Short History of Some Discoveries in Atomic Physics*, which describes for the layman this century's advances in fundamental physics.

ARNOLD PACEY ON TECHNOLOGY

The Way Things Work by David Macaulay and Neil Ardley. One of the best of many illustrated books on machines and inventions, this will help with the most basic kind of understanding about how various mechanisms function.

Design for the Real World: Human Ecology and Social Change by Victor Papanek. Another aspect of understanding technology is to understand how inventors and engineers approach their work. This book is partly about that, but mainly about how inventors and designers ought to be thinking if they want to serve the real needs of ordinary people.

The Existential Pleasures of Engineering by Samuel C. Florman. Here is a very different view of how inventors and engineers think, written by a practicing engineer who finds artistic and religious experience in his work.

The Evolution of Technology by George Basalla. This book offers an original and important historical view of the human impulse to invention and the sources of progress in technology. It argues that necessity is not often the mother of invention and that playfulness, fantasy, and imagination are more important.

Technology and American Economic Growth by Nathan Rosenberg. An economist's view of the development of technology offers a different perspective on the history and origin of inventions and their role in society.

A Short History of Twentieth Century Technology,

1900-1950 by Trevor I. Williams. This is a comprehensive, factual, but perhaps rather dry, account of developments in technology during the first half of the century.

More Work for Mother: The Ironies of Household Technology from the Open Hearth to the Microwave by Ruth Schwartz Cowan. Of particular value for its perspective on 20th-century technology, interpretations offered here show that social expectations and the organization of daily life alter the significance of some inventions in surprising ways.

High-Tech Society by Tom Forester. This nicely rounded survey of the computer revolution and information technology examines the social implications of these very modern technologies as they appeared in the mid-1980s, and will still seem largely relevant.

The Nuclear Barons by Peter Pringle and James Spigelman. Here is yet another aspect of the story of modern technology, told in a frankly hostile, but accurate and readable manner.

Mastering the Machine: Poverty, Aid and Technology by Ian Smillie. Some people feel that the biggest danger associated with modern technology and the way it is used is the impact on the environment. Others feel that a bigger problem is the fact that two-thirds of the human race live in poverty, many on the edge of starvation. These problems are interrelated and present an opportunity to show what technology might achieve. But this book points out the dangers of thinking only in terms of hardware, and advocates an approach based on people-centered thinking.

The Whale and the Reactor: A Search for Limits in an

Age of Technology by Langdon Winner. This is an important, thoughtful book on the role of technology in modern society. It mentions political, social, and environmental implications of how we use technology, and asks how ethical constraints and social controls might be developed.

ARNOLD PACEY is a lecturer and writer on technology. His books include *The Maze of Ingenuity: Ideas and Idealism in the Development of Technology*; *Technology in World Civilization*; and *The Culture of Technology.*

We have to decide fairly soon what it is we as humans
ought to become, because we are on the brink
of having the power to create any experience we desire.
— Howard Rheingold, *Virtual Reality*

HERBERT SIMON ON ARTIFICIAL INTELLIGENCE

My interests in artificial intelligence have to do primarily with its use in psychology — in understanding human thinking.

Machinery of the Mind by George Johnson. A generally reliable and very readable popular account of this controversial field.

Machines Who Think by Pamela McCorduck. For readers who like biography and history, an excellent and reliable account of the history of the field, based on extensive interviews with almost all the actors.

Artificial Intelligence by Elaine Rich. One of the best, and most readable, introductory textbooks.

HERBERT A. SIMON is professor of psychology at Carnegie Mellon University. He is the author of *The Sciences of the Artificial* and *Models of My Life*, an autobiography that also examines artificial intelligence and its role in the cognitive revolution in psychology.

CHAPTER 7
BUSINESS

It is clear that success in business is both an art and a science, with plenty of good luck and good sense thrown in. Here, those who are successful in business share the sometimes surprising sources of their inspiration. And no less an authority than John Kenneth Galbraith challenges us with his titles on economics. Just try to make it through this chapter without making a mental note to read Adam Smith.

WALLY AMOS ON INSPIRATION AND MOTIVATION

Love Is Letting Go of Fear by Jerry Jampolsky, M.D.
The Greatest Salesman in the World by Og Mandino.
Think and Grow Rich by Napoleon Hill.
You'll See It When You Believe It by Dr. Wayne Dyer.
Man's Search For Meaning by Viktor E. Frankl, M.D.

These five books will give you insight into love, caring, forgiveness, faith, and all the other positive characteristics of life. Reading them will change you and your life for the better.

WALLY AMOS is owner and president of Famous Amos Chocolate Chip Cookies. He was formerly a talent agent at the William Morris Agency, where he represented The Temptations, The Supremes, Marvin Gaye, and Dionne Warwick. He is the author of *The Famous Amos Story: The Face that Launched a Thousand Chips*.

WARREN BENNIS ON MANAGEMENT

Management by Peter Drucker.
Leadership by James MacGregor Burns.

WARREN BENNIS is Distinguished Professor of Business Administration at the University of Southern California, and the author of eighteen books on business leadership and organizational dynamics, including *On Becoming a Leader*; *Leaders*; and *Why Leaders Can't Lead*.

Leadership is the lifting of a man's vision to higher sights, the raising of a man's performance to a higher standard, the building of a man's personality beyond its normal limitations.
— Peter Drucker, *Management*

CHRISTINE HEFNER

Leadership Is an Art by Max De Pree.
When Giants Learn to Dance by Rosabeth Moss Kanter.

CHRISTINE A. HEFNER is chairman and chief executive officer of Playboy Enterprises. She joined the media company in 1974.

AL RIES AND JACK TROUT ON MARKETING

Reality in Advertising by Rosser Reeves. The essence of marketing is "communications." This is the basic communications bible, admittedly expressed in terms of the big-time advertising agency. You don't have to be an advertiser, however, to utilize the power of Rosser Reeves's strategic ideas.

Confessions of an Advertising Man by David Ogilvy. If you can filter out the author's egocentricities, you'll learn how to structure your communications to get into the mind of the prospect. David Ogilvy is the world's best copywriter. Just reading this book will improve your own writing style.

Up the Organization! by Robert Townsend. This book complements the Reeves and Ogilvy volumes. It outlines the marketing function from the point of view of the advertiser rather than the advertising agency. In particular, Townsend makes the case for a rational, "detached" modus operandi.

MaxiMarketing by Stan Rapp and Tom Collins. The next

plateau for marketing will involve the computer. Stan Rapp and Tom Collins outline what the future will be like for marketers who make maxi use of the new computing technologies.

AL RIES is founder and chairman and JACK TROUT is president of Trout & Ries, a marketing strategy firm whose clients have included IBM, Xerox, Chase Manhattan Bank, and Burger King. They are co-authors of *Positioning: The Battle for Your Mind*; *Marketing Warfare*; and *Horse Sense: How to Pull Ahead on the Business Track*.

ALBERT SHANKER ON LABOR

Harriette Arnow, **The Dollmaker**
Wayne Broehl, Jr., **The Molly Maguires**
Stanley Buder, **Pullman: An Experiment in Industrial Order and Community Planning, 1880-1930**
William Cahn, **Lawrence, 1912: The Bread and Roses Strike**
Charles Denby, **Indignant Heart: A Black Worker's Journal**
John Dos Passos, **U.S.A.**
Foster R. Dulles and Melvyn Dubofsky, **Labor in America: A History**, 4th edition
John G. Dunne, **Delano: The Story of the California Grape Strike**
Richard B. Freeman and James L. Medoff, **What Do Unions Do?**

James Green, **The World of the Worker: Labor in 20th Century America**
Jacob Riis, **How the Other Half Lives: Studies Among the Tenements of New York**
Upton Sinclair, **The Jungle**
John Spargo, **The Bitter Cry of the Children**
Wallace Stegner, **Joe Hill**
John Steinbeck, **In Dubious Battle** and **The Grapes of Wrath**
Irving Stone, **Clarence Darrow for the Defense: A Biography**
Studs Terkel, **Working**
Barbara Wertheimer, **We Were There: The Story of Working Women in America**
Robert Zieger, **John L. Lewis: Labor Leader**

ALBERT SHANKER is the longtime president of the American Federation of Teachers, a national teachers union, and serves on the AFL-CIO Executive Council.

ANDREW TOBIAS ON INVESTMENT

Extraordinary Popular Delusions and the Madness of Crowds by Charles Mackay, published in 1841 and in print ever since. Fun to read, although you can skip a few hundred pages about alchemists — it's the first 100 pages or so that any investor ought to read before placing his bets.

The Intelligent Investor by Benjamin Graham. The bible of Graham students such as Warren Buffet, though more nuts, bolts, and accounting than any others on my list.

The Money Game by Adam Smith. A classic bit of not-so-distant history.

Where Are the Customers' Yachts? by Fred Schwed. A wonderfully funny send-up of stockbrokers that, at the same time, gives you a flavor of Wall Street in the era before Adam Smith's *The Money Game*. This one is hard to find.

A Random Walk Down Wall Street by Burton Malkiel, 5th edition. A nice mix between fun and analytical, it should surely persuade you to invest through no-load mutual funds rather than throw the darts yourself.

ANDREW TOBIAS is the author of several books on investment, including *The Invisible Bankers*; *The Only Investment Guide You'll Ever Need*; *Money Angles*; and *Auto Insurance Alert!: Why the System Stinks, How to Fix It, and What to Do in the Meantime.*

GAIL FOSLER ON ECONOMICS

The U.S. Economy Demystified by Albert Summers. What the major economic statistics mean and their significance for business.

How We Live by Victor Fuchs. Cuts through pop panaceas to get to innovative solutions to contemporary problems — not just about economics.

The Worldly Philosophers by Robert Heilbroner. Kind of a people approach to economics.

GAIL D. FOSLER is an economist at the Conference Board, a business trade group.

JOHN KENNETH GALBRAITH ON ECONOMICS

The three books which are indispensable in economics are Adam Smith's **The Nature and Causes of the Wealth of Nations**, a brilliantly written book and a tract for all time. It is much celebrated by the ministry of the righteous right, few of whom have read it. Were they to do so — disapproval of the corporate form, approval of a wealth tax — they would be greatly shocked.

The second volume would, of course, be Thorstein Veblen's **Theory of the Leisure Class**. This is one of the great documents in American social history. In treating the American rich as though they were an anthropological counterpart of Polynesian tribal rites, Veblen not only set records for annoyance but left the phrases "conspicuous consumption" and "conspicuous waste" for all time.

The third indispensable volume is John Maynard Keynes's **General Theory of Employment, Interest, and Money**. This initiated the Keynesian Revolution, which made governments responsible, as they remain to this day, for the level of employment, general well-being, and economic growth in the economy.

Those who have read these three books will not have the total of economics, but anyone who has not read any of them is truly devoid.

JOHN KENNETH GALBRAITH is an economist and teacher. He is the author of more than a score of books, including *The Affluent Society*, *The Age of Uncertainty*, *The Culture of Contentment*, and *The World Economy Since the Wars*. He taught economics at Harvard University from 1948 until his retirement in 1975. He served as U.S. ambassador to India under President Kennedy.

LESTER THUROW ON ECONOMICS

The Making of Economic Society by Robert Heilbroner.
The Great Crash of 1929 by John Kenneth Galbraith.
British Factory, Japanese Factory by Ronald Dore.
Barbarians at the Gate by Bryan Burrough and John Helyar.
The United States and World Economy: From Bretton Woods To the Bush Team by Walter Meade.

LESTER C. THUROW is dean of the Alfred P. Sloan School of Management at MIT and the author of more than a dozen books on economics. His books include *The Zero-Sum Society*, *The Zero-Sum Solution*, and *Generating Inequality*.

CHAPTER 8
HISTORY

Historians have always played a crucial role in society, recording and reflecting a culture's identity through the ages. Here contributors who are among the world's most noted historians (say, Arthur Schlesinger) rub elbows with others, like Howard Fast, who have borne witness to history in notable ways. Together, they provide an extraordinary introduction to the vast literature of world history from Thucydides' *Peloponnesian War* to *The Making of the Atomic Bomb*. What makes these lists so fascinating is the way in which authoritative overviews — Gibbon's *Decline and Fall of the Roman Empire*, Sowell's *Ethnic America* — are balanced by evocative captured moments in time, whether it be a view of the war, marriage and German Nazi resistance through *Letters to Freya*, or America's racial conflicts in Steinbeck's *Travels with Charlie*.

MICHAEL GRANT ON ANCIENT HISTORY

Edward Gibbon, **The Decline and Fall of the Roman Empire**, published from 1776 to 1788
Ronald Syme, **The Roman Revolution**
Maurice Bowra, **The Greek Experience**

MICHAEL GRANT, a former fellow at Trinity College in Cambridge, England, is the author of more than 30 books on the ancient world. His books include *History of Rome*, *The Rise of the Greeks*, *The Ancient Mediterranean*, *The Fall of the Roman Empire*, and *Anthology of Classic Historians.*

History is little more than the register of the crimes,
follies, and misfortunes of mankind.
— Edward Gibbon, *The Decline and Fall of the Roman Empire*

ROBERT BARTLETT ON MEDIEVAL HISTORY

Feudal Society by Marc Bloch (English translation). A classic work, especially valuable for its picture of the social structure and culture of the aristocracy.

From Memory to Written Record: England 1066-1307 by Michael Clanchy. A detailed and stimulating study of the impact of literacy on an oral society.

Conquest, Coexistence and Change: Wales 1063-1415 by Rees Davies. The tale of a small country faced with large-scale social changes and a powerful, hostile neighbor.

Rural Economy and Country Life in the Medieval West by Georges Duby. A masterly survey of the life of the countryside, the basis of medieval life.

A History of the Crusades by Steven Runciman (3 volumes). A leisurely and vivid narrative of one of the most spectacular religious and military movements of the medieval period.

The Making of the Middle Ages by Richard W. Southern. A book that illuminates the life of the 11th and 12th centuries from the experience of those who lived at that time; indispensable.

ROBERT J. BARTLETT is a professor of medieval history at the University of Chicago. He is author of *Trial by Fire and Water: The Medieval Judicial Order* and *The Making of Europe: Conquest, Colonization and Cultural Change in Europe 930-1350.*

ANTHONY GRAFTON ON RENAISSANCE HISTORY

The Civilization of the Renaissance in Italy by Jacob Burckhardt. The great evocation of a period in Western cultural history, without forerunner and more evocative than any successor.

The Crisis of the Early Italian Renaissance by Hans Baron. A brilliant effort to connect political with intellectual history in 15th century Florence.

Renaissance Thought and Its Sources by Paul Kristeller. The best survey of Renaissance scholarship and philosophy; lucid, lively, astonishingly comprehensive.

Painting and Experience in 15th Century Italy by Michael Baxandall. A penetrating essay on the social and economic origins of Renaissance art.

ANTHONY J. GRAFTON is a professor of history at Princeton University, and the author, with Lisa Jardine, of *From Humanism to the Humanities.*

ROBERT DARNTON ON THE ENLIGHTENMENT

In order to taste the flavor of the Enlightenment and its surrounding culture, I would recommend that readers take up these three books, which are accessible, enjoyable, and enlightening:

Montesquieu, **Persian Letters**
Voltaire, **Candide**
Benjamin Franklin, **The Autobiography of Benjamin Franklin**

ROBERT DARNTON is a professor of history at Princeton University and a MacArthur fellow. His book, *The Great Cat Massacre and Other Episodes in French Culture*, won the Los Angeles Times Prize in history.

VOLKER BERGHAHN ON NAZISM

Ian Kershaw, **The Nazi Dictatorship**, 2nd edition. Best guide to the debate on the basic character of the Third Reich and its regime. Concise, with helpful "evaluations" at the end of each chapter.

Joachim C. Fest, **Hitler**. Major biography of Hitler. Somewhat unbalanced in that it is more concerned with the rise of Hitler than his years in power. But beautifully written and attempting to relate the individual to his times.

Renate Bridenthal, et al., editors, **When Biology Became Destiny**. Important collection of essays by historians of German women. Looks not merely at the situation of women under Nazism, but also provides a good deal of background by examining the experience of the 1920s.

Helmuth von Moltke, B. Ruhm von Oppen editor and translator, **Letters to Freya**. Wartime letters to his wife by one of the intellectual leaders of the underground resistance to Nazism. Shows both the frustrations and agonies of an upright man and what dictatorship and war did to the mentalities of ordinary Germans.

VOLKER BERGHAHN teaches history at Brown University and is the author of *Modern Germany: Society, Economy and Politics in the 20th Century.*

JOHN DOWER ON WORLD WAR II

Three general studies introduce the vast sweep of the war: **The Second World War** by John Keegan, **Total War: Causes and Courses of the Second World War** by Peter Calvocoressi, Guy Wint, and John Pritchard, 2nd edition, and **The Issue of War: States, Societies, and the Far Eastern Conflict of 1941-45** by Christopher Thorne. Ultimately, however, it is the voices of ordinary men and women engulfed by the war which most memorably recreate these terrible years.

The Good War by Studs Terkel is an engrossing oral history, and has a stunning complement from the Japanese side in **Japan at War** by Haruko Taya Cook and Theodore Cook.

Survival in Auschwitz by Primo Levi is a classic among the vast literature on the Holocaust.

Fires on the Plain by Shohei Ooka, based on the author's experience as a soldier, is the most searing Japanese novel to emerge out of the war. Its American counterpart in evoking the horror of war in the Pacific theater is Norman Mailer's first novel, **The Naked and the Dead**.

Two of the finest American combat memoirs also focus on the Pacific War: **Goodbye, Darkness** by William Manchester and **With the Old Breed at Peleliu and Okinawa** by Eugene B. Sledge.

Black Rain by Masuji Ibuse, inspired by a diary kept at the time, is an intimate account of the human legacy of Hiroshima. It provides an essential counterpoint to the excellent analysis of the decision to develop and use the atomic bomb presented in Martin Sherwin's **A World Destroyed: The Atomic Bomb and the Grand Alliance**.

JOHN W. DOWER is the Henry Lee Professor of International Cooperation at the Massachusetts Institute of Technology. His books include *Empire and Aftermath: Yoshida Shigeru and the Japanese Experience, 1878-1954* and *War Without Mercy: Race and Power in the Pacific War.*

PAUL FUSSELL ON WORLD WAR I

Three general overviews of World War I should be mentioned:

My own **The Great War and Modern Memory**
Modris Ekstein, **Rites of Spring: The Great War & the Birth of the Modern World**
Samuel Hynes, **A War Imagined: The First World War and English Culture**

Then there is Eric J. Leed's **No Man's Land: Combat and Identity in World War I**, an interesting psychological inquiry into what it felt like to be a Great War soldier.

Martin Middlebrook's **The First Day on the Somme** is an unforgettable, thorough account of one of the 20th century's worst battles.

The on-the-spot memoirists should not be overlooked:

Frank Richards, **Old Soldiers Never Die**
Siegfried Sassoon, **The Memoirs of George Scherston**
Edmund Blunden, **Undertones of War**
Robert Graves, **Good-bye to All That**. The masterpiece of them all.

The war generated a vast amount of protest poetry:

Wilfred Owen, **Collected Poems**
Siegfried Sassoon, **Collected Poems**
Ivor Gurney, **Poems**

PAUL FUSSELL is a professor of English literature at the University of Pennsylvania. His book, *The Great War and Modern Memory*, won a National Book Award. His other books include *Samuel Johnson, The Life of Writing,* and *Class: A Guide through the American Status System.*

Soldiers are citizens of death's grey land,
Drawing no dividend from time's tomorrows.
— Siegfried Sassoon

PETER HAYES ON NAZISM

The best overviews:

The German Dictatorship by Karl Dietrich Bracher. Heavy-going and gradually becoming dated, this nonetheless remains the finest, most profound survey in English.

Nazism: A History in Documents and Eyewitness Accounts, edited by Jeremy Noakes and Geoffrey Pridham (2 volumes). An excellent compendium of materials that bring the reader close to the actual experience of the time.

Life in the Third Reich, edited by Richard Bessel. A compact collection of highly readable topical essays by some of today's leading specialists.

The Meaning of Hitler by Sebastian Haffner. An elegantly written, penetrating, and occasionally wrong-headed book that will (and deserves to) fascinate general readers.

The Nazi Dictatorship by Ian Kershaw. Though weak on the economy, this is an intelligent and up-to-date guide to historical research and differences of interpretation.

Important works on specific topics:

The Nazi Seizure of Power by William Sheridan Allen. A wonderfully written and structured account of the Nazi rise to power as seen through the prism of a single small town.

Hitler's World View by Eberhard Jackel. Concise and lucid, this is a superb analysis of the ideology that drove the Nazi Fuhrer.

Hitler's Social Revolution by David Schoenbaum. A minor historical classic, which brilliantly analyzes the relationship between ideology and practice in the Third Reich and the unintended effects of that regime on modern Germany.

The Hitler Myth and **Popular Opinion and Politcal Dissent in the Third Reich** by Ian Kershaw. A pair of books that provide the most balanced and reliable assessments of what Germans actually thought under Hitler.

Nazi Economics by Avraham Barkai. The best available explanation of Nazi economic ideology and its consequences.

The Nazi Economic Recovery 1932-38 and **Goering, the**

"Iron Man" by Richard Overy. Together these works offer the most up-to-date treatment of Nazi economic practice.

Hitler's Army by Omer Bartov. A perceptive demonstration of the barbarizing impact of Nazi ideology on German military conduct, especially on the Eastern Front, and on German society.

Unanswered Questions, edited by Francois Furet. The best available collection of experts' responses to the most frequently asked questions concerning the Nazi onslaught against the Jews.

The Holocaust in History by Michael Marrus. A first-rate analytical survey of historical writing on the Holocaust.

PETER HAYES teaches history and German at Northwestern University and is the author of *Industry and Ideology: IG Farben in the Nazi Era*.

ADAM ULAM ON STALINISM

Roy Medvedev, **Let History Judge: The Origins and Consequences of Stalinism**

Robert Conquest, **The Great Terror: A Reassessment**; **The Great Terror: Stalin's Purge of the '30s**; **The Harvest of Sorrow: Soviet Collectivization and the Terror-Famine**; and **Stalin: Breaker of Nations**

Isaac Deutscher, **The Great Purges** and **Stalin: A Political Biography**

Robert Tucker, **Stalin in Power: The Revolution from Above**

Walter Laqueur, **Stalin: The Glasnost Revelations**
John Scott, **Behind the Urals: An American Worker in Russia's City of Steel**
Nikita S. Khrushchev, **The Anatomy of Terror: Khrushchev's Revelations About Stalin's Regime**
Aleksandr I. Solzhenitsyn, **The First Circle**
Adam Ulam, **Stalin**

ADAM B. ULAM is a professor of government at Harvard University, and the director of its Russian Research Center. He is the author of numerous books on the Soviet Union, including *Dangerous Relations: The Soviet Union in World Politics 1970-1982* and *The Kirov Affair.*

DAVID WYMAN ON THE HOLOCAUST

The Destruction of the European Jews by Raul Hilberg. The most important overview of the Holocaust.
Night by Elie Wiesel and **Survival in Auschwitz** by Primo Levi. Auschwitz as experienced by two Jews who survived it.
On Both Sides of the Wall by Vladka Meed. An autobiographical account of the Warsaw Ghetto and the Jewish resistance there.
The Diary of a Young Girl by Anne Frank.

DAVID S. WYMAN is an historian who teaches at the University of Massachusetts at Amherst. He is the author of *The Abandonment of the Jews, 1941-45* and editor of the 13-volume *America and the Holocaust.*

LINDA CHAVEZ ON IMMIGRATION

How the Other Half Lives by Jacob Riis is probably the best examination of life in the urban slums where many immigrants resided in the early part of this century. To anyone who thinks earlier waves of immigrants encountered greater opportunities and less discrimination than those coming here today from Latin America and Asia, Riis's book is a reminder that life has never been easy for newcomers.

Hunger of Memory by Richard Rodriguez is not technically an "immigrant" book since the author is American-born. Nonetheless, Rodriguez gives a poignant description of his own transition from his Spanish-speaking home, bound by the love and tradition of his immigrant parents, to the English-speaking world of school and public life. In doing so he captures the pain many first-generation Americans endure as they bridge the cultural chasm between their parents' experiences of the new world and their own.

Beyond the Melting Pot by Nathan Glazer and Daniel P. Moynihan remains the classic text on the integration of major ethnic groups in the United States. Although the book was written 30 years ago and deals specifically with New York City, its lessons on the tenacity of ethnic identity still holds true today.

Ethnic America by Thomas Sowell focuses on the range of experiences of different ethnic groups as they assimilated into the social, political, and economic mainstream. Sowell's thesis is that no single "immigrant experience" defines groups as diverse as the Chinese and Puerto Ricans. Among the factors that affect immigrants' adaptation to life in America, which Sowell richly describes, are the time and place of their arrival and the unique history and culture immigrants bring with them to these shores.

LINDA CHAVEZ was staff director of the U.S. Commission on Civil Rights from 1983 to 1985 and director of public liaison under President Reagan. She was also the president of U.S. English, an organization dealing with language policy from 1987 to 1988. She is author of *Out of the Barrio: Toward a New Politics of Hispanic Assimilation*.

EVAN S. CONNELL ON THE FRONTIER

On the Border with Crook by John G. Bourke.
Massacres of the Mountains by J.P. Dunn.
A Century of Dishonor by Helen Hunt Jackson.
Forty Miles a Day on Beans and Hay by Don Rickey.
Army Life in Dakota by Philippe Regis de Trobriand.

EVAN S. CONNELL is a novelist. His books include *Son of the Morning Star: Custer and the Little Bighorn* and *Mrs. Bridge.*

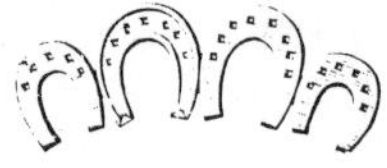

RICHARD W. ETULAIN ON THE FRONTIER

General overviews:

The Frontier in American History by Frederick Jackson Turner.
The Great Plains by Walter Prescott Webb.
Virgin Land: The American West as Symbol and Myth by Henry Nash Smith.
The Reader's Encyclopedia of the American West, edited by Howard R. Lamar.
Westward Expansion by Ray A. Billington and Martin Ridge, 5th edition.
Legacy of Conquest by Patricia Nelson Limerick.
It's Your Misfortune and None of My Own: A New

History of the American West by Richard White.

Topical volumes:

Frontier Women: The Trans-Mississippi West 1840-1880 by Julie Roy Jeffrey.

The Great Father: The United States Government and the American Indians by Francis Paul Prucha (2 volumes).

Rivers of Empire: Water, Aridity and the Growth of the American West by Donald Worster.

The West of the Imagination by William H. Goetzmann and William N. Goetzmann.

Cadillac Desert: The American West and Its Disappearing Water by Marc Reisner.

The American West as Living Space by Wallace Stegner.

Occupied America: A History of Chicanos by Rodolfo Acuna, 3rd edition.

Growing Up with the Country: Childhood on the Far Western Frontier by Elliott West.

Western literature:

The Virginian by Owen Wister.

My Antonia by Willa Cather.

Grapes of Wrath by John Steinbeck.

House Made of Dawn by N. Scott Momaday.

Play It As It Lays by Joan Didion.

Angle of Repose by Wallace Stegner.

Lonesome Dove by Larry McMurtry.

Prose and Poetry of the American West, edited by James C. Work.

RICHARD W. ETULAIN teaches the history and culture of the American West at the University of New Mexico. With Michael P. Malone, he is the author of *The American West: A Twentieth Century History.*

HOWARD FAST ON McCARTHYISM

There are only four books I would select and recommend for a comprehensive understanding of the McCarthy period. Of course, I speak from the point of view of one of those attacked during that time, a person who suffered severely in terms of my profession as well as physically and psychologically. Yet even putting that aside, these are the only four books I know of that give a clear and (by my belief) unbiased picture of the time.

Being Red by Howard Fast (memoir).
The Pledge by Howard Fast (fiction).
Naming Names by Victor S. Navasky (history).
Scoundrel Time by Lillian Hellman (memoir).

There are many other books that touch on this subject, dealing with the times and the Communist Party. But I feel these bear most directly on the subject.

HOWARD FAST is the author of more than 80 books, including the historical novels *Citizen Tom Paine*, *Freedom Road*, and *Spartacus*, as well as the five-volume series *The Immigrants*. After refusing to cooperate with the House Un-American Activities Committee, he was blacklisted from 1950 to 1960.

ROGER A. FISCHER ON AMERICAN HISTORY

To gain an understanding of the American heritage is no simple task, for the reader must delve beyond the major milestones of "official" history to explore the complexities and contradictions, the experiences and ideals of the diverse elements that comprise the American family. Books published on the subject would fill many miles of library shelves. For me and for my students over three decades, these 20 volumes stand out as especially helpful for gaining a true understanding of the American experience. Along with scholarly studies, they include autobiographical memoirs and literary masterworks, possessing in common only the genius of insight into the soul of our heritage as Americans.

William Bradford, **Of Plymouth Plantation**, edited by Samuel Eliot Morrison. A crisp, insightful memoir of the daily struggles of the Pilgrim pioneers to found and sustain the Plymouth colony.

Daniel Boorstin, **The Americans: The Colonial Experience**. A demanding but compelling synthesis of the genesis of a uniquely American culture and way of thinking during the colonial period.

Benjamin Franklin, **Autobiography**. The informative and

entertaining reminiscences of America's premier Enlightenment thinker and world citizen.

Garry Wills, **Inventing America**. A cogent study of the mind of Thomas Jefferson and the philosophical foundations of the Declaration of Independence.

Alexis de Tocqueville, **Democracy in America**. A brilliant analysis of early American political culture by a young French aristocrat.

Walter Lord, **A Time to Stand**. A stirring, superbly written account of the fall of the Alamo and the birth of the Texas Republic.

Frederick Douglass, **Life and Times of Frederick Douglass**. The inspiring, uncompromising memoir of the renowned Douglass is considered by many to be the finest treatise on human liberty written by any American.

James M. McPherson, **Ordeal by Fire**. The most lucid single-volume study of the causes, course, and consequences of the American Civil War.

Oscar Handlin, **The Uprooted**, revised edition. An engaging synthesis of the immigrant experience from the immigrant viewpoint.

Mark Twain, **The Adventures of Huckleberry Finn**. After more than a century, Twain's beloved saga of the river and the raft remains the most quintessentially American of all writings and, arguably, the finest of all American literary masterworks.

Dee Brown, **Bury My Heart at Wounded Knee**. A compelling, moving account of the infamous Wounded Knee massacre and the passing of a proud Indian tradition of resistance.

Willa Cather, **My Antonia**. A splendid novel unrivaled in its portrayal of pioneer life on the Western prairie and the strength of character required to survive.

Henry Adams, **The Education of Henry Adams**. A challenging memoir by the scion of America's most distinguished public family, keenly perceptive in its analysis of the changes confronting American culture as a result of the Industrial Revolution.

Studs Terkel, **Hard Times**. An engaging oral history of the 1930s, a look at the troubled Depression decade through the thoughts and words of its victims.

Edwin O'Connor, **The Last Hurrah**. Arguably the best recent American novel and a splendid study of the politics and political culture of the changing American city.

Roger Kahn, **The Boys of Summer**. A superbly written, moving boyhood reminiscence of the 1955-56 Brooklyn Dodgers; probably the finest essay on American sports or American heroes ever written.

John Steinbeck, **Travels with Charlie**. A fascinating yet disturbing narrative of the travels of the novelist and his elderly poodle through a nation beset with racial conflict.

Anne Moody, **Coming of Age in Mississippi**. The refreshingly candid memoir of an indomitable young Mississippian whose rite-of-passage to womanhood came as a volunteer in the Civil Rights movement.

Daniel Boorstin, **The Image: Or What Happened to the American Dream**. A brilliant, alarming analysis of modern media culture and its confusion of reality and image, heroes and celebrities, and events and pseudo-events.

Arthur M. Schlesinger, Jr., **The Imperial Presidency**. A provocative, persuasive study of the unchecked growth in the power of the American presidency leading to Vietnam and Watergate.

ROGER A. FISCHER is a professor of history at the University of Minnesota at Duluth. His books include *The Segregation Struggle*; *Tippecanoe and Trinkets Too: Material Culture in American Presidential Campaigns*; and *Them Damned Pictures: Explorations in American Political Cartoon Art*.

JOHN KERRY ON THE VIETNAM WAR

Advice and Support: The Early Years of the U.S. Army in Vietnam, 1941-1960 by Ronald H. Spector. A detailed account of how the American military establishment became inextricably involved in Vietnam after World War II.

The Irony of Vietnam: The System Worked by Leslie H. Gelb with Richard K. Betts. A point-by-point analysis of America's grand strategy, which made involvement in Vietnam inevitable.

The Communist Road to Power in Vietnam by William J. Duiker. A unique description of how Communist ascendancy in Vietnam evolved from nationalist sentiments and how the Communists skillfully infiltrated their cadres into South Vietnam during the war.

America's Longest War: The United States and

Vietnam, 1950-1975 by George C. Herring. A comprehensive yet manageable primer on the political and military aspects of America's war effort in Southeast Asia.

War Comes to Long An: Revolutionary Conflict in a Vietnamese Province by Jeffrey Race. A unique view of how the war affected a particular strategically located province in South Vietnam.

Without Honor: Defeat in Vietnam and Cambodia by Arnold R. Isaacs. A detailed account of the United States' political and military strategies which caused South Vietnam to fall in 1975.

The Best and the Brightest by David Halberstam. The authoritative account of the motivations and strategies of the individuals who initiated and expanded America's involvement in Vietnam.

On Strategy: A Critical Analysis of the Vietnam War by Col. Harry G. Summers, Jr. An extremely concise and lucid analysis of the strategic miscalculations which led to America's defeat in Vietnam.

A Bright Shining Lie: John Paul Vann and America in Vietnam by Neil Sheehan. A compelling analysis of the U.S. war effort in Vietnam through the life and death of the American who probably knew the country as well as any other, Col. John Paul Vann.

JOHN KERRY has served in the U.S. Senate as a Democrat from Massachusetts since 1985. He was a Navy officer who served in combat during the Vietnam War and later organized Vietnam Veterans Against the War.

JAMES M. McPHERSON ON THE CIVIL WAR

The Confederate Nation 1861-1865 by Emory M. Thomas. A one-volume narrative covering the causes of the war as well as all aspects of the war itself.

"A People's Contest": The Union and Civil War 1861-1865 by Phillip S. Paludan. The most succinct history of the Union home front.

The War for the Union by Allan Nevins (4 volumes). The fullest account of the war on the battle front and the home front; especially good on the North.

The Centennial History of the Civil War by Bruce Catton (3 volumes). A readable narrative emphasizing military aspects of the war.

The Civil War: A Narrative by Shelby Foote (3 volumes). A rich, full, and fast-paced narrative of the military history of the war.

The Civil War: An Illustrated History by Geoffrey C. Ward with Ric Burns and Ken Burns. The lavishly illustrated volume which accompanied the PBS documentary on the Civil War.

JAMES M. MCPHERSON is a professor of history at Princeton University. His book, *Battle Cry of Freedom: The Civil War Era* won the Pulitzer Prize for history. His other works include *Ordeal by Fire: Civil War and Reconstruction* and *The Negro's Civil War.*

EDMUND MORGAN ON THE AMERICAN REVOLUTION

The Ideological Origins of the American Revolution by Bernard Bailyn. The book that has done most to shape modern understanding of the causes of the Revolution.

The Creation of the American Republic, 1776-1787 by Gordon Wood. The book which has done the most to shape modern understanding of the effects of the Revolution.

The Glorious Cause: The American Revolution, 1763-1789 by Robert Middlekauff. The best overall narrative account of the Revolution.

EDMUND MORGAN is professor emeritus at Yale University, where he taught American history for more than 30 years. His many books include *The Birth of the Republic*, *The Meaning of Independence*, and *The Genius of George Washington*.

PETER ROSE ON IMMIGRATION

I offer a dozen titles on immigration and the character of this "nation of immigrants."

Richard Alba, **Ethnic Identity**. A stimulating assessment of the twilight-of-ethnicity debate, with particular focus on European immigrants and their descendants.

Roger Daniels, **Coming to America**. A general history of immigration and ethnicity in American life by an historian best known for his writings on the experiences of Asian-Americans.

Lawrence H. Fuchs, **The American Kaleidoscope: Race, Ethnicity and the Civic Culture**. One of the foremost experts on U.S. immigration and former executive director of the Select Commission on Immigration and Refugee Policy under President Carter, Fuchs's encyclopedic book describes various patterns of migration and of pluralism (voluntary, coercive, etc.) in the United States.

Nathan Glazer, editor, **Clamor at the Gates**. A collection of original essays by social scientists on the post-1965 immigration.

Peter Kivisto and Dag Blanck, editors, **American Immigrants and Their Generations**. Studies and commentaries on "Hansen's Law" about immigrants and their children ("What the son wishes to forget, the grandson wishes to remember.")

Gilburt Loescher and John Scanlan, **Calculated Kindness**.

A study in the politics of rescue and America's refugee policies by a political scientist and specialist on immigration law.

Arthur Mann, **The One and the Many**. A noted historian examines ethnic diversity and American identity in this stimulating and prescient volume.

Alejandro Portes and Ruben Rumbaut, **Immigrant America**. Two sociologists assess the changing character of American immigration, highlighting such issues as acculturation, economic adaptation, language acquisition, and both physical and social mobility.

David Reimers, **Still the Golden Door**. (Subtitled "The Third World Comes to America.") The author, an historian, discusses the demographic shifts that occurred as a result of the passage of the Immigration Act of 1965 and the implications of "The New Immigration."

Rita J. Simon, **Public Opinion and the Immigrant**. This is an examination of images of and attitudes toward immigrants as reflected in American print media in the period 1880-1980. The author, a sociologist, is president of the American Immigration Institute.

Ronald Takaki, **Strangers from a Different Shore**. A lively and detailed history of Americans from Asia showing both common and diverse experiences of those from China, Japan, Korea, the Philippines, India, and other nearby countries.

Norman and Naomi Zucker, **The Guarded Gate**. An examination of the unique status — and unique problems — of refugees in the context of American policies which, according to the authors, have been driven more by political than humanitarian concerns.

PETER I. ROSE is a professor of sociology and anthropology at Smith College, and the author of many books on sociology, including *They and We; The Subject is Race;* and *Sociology*. He also edited *The Study of Society*.

ARTHUR M. SCHLESINGER, JR. ON AMERICAN HISTORY

Here is a list of books I think Americans should read to achieve "cultural literacy" about our nation.

Emerson's Essays
Abraham Lincoln, **Speeches and Writings**
Alexis de Tocqueville, **Democracy in America**
James Bryce, **The American Commonwealth**
Reinhold Niebuhr, **The Irony of American History**
Edmund Wilson, editor, **The Shock of Recognition**
Gunnar Myrdal, **An American Dilemma**

Herbert Croly, **The Promise of American Life**
William James, **Pragmatism**
Henry Adams, **The Education of Henry Adams**
H.L. Mencken, **The American Language**

ARTHUR M. SCHLESINGER, Jr. is Albert Schweitzer Professor of the Humanities at the City University of New York. He has won the Pulitzer Prizes for history and biography and the National Book Award twice. His works include *The Age of Jackson*; *A Thousand Days: John F. Kennedy in the White House*; *The Imperial Presidency*; *The Cycles of American History*; and *The Disuniting of America.*

Man is explicable by nothing less than all his history.
— Ralph Waldo Emerson, *Emerson's Essays*

EMORY M. THOMAS ON THE CIVIL WAR

An American Iliad: The Story of the Civil War by Charles P. Roland is the best brief book on the war period. Roland's brevity possesses both soul and wit.

Victims: A True Story of the Civil War by Phillip Shaw Paludan is an older book, but a very important work. Paludan relates the story of a massacre in western North Carolina and offers insight and understanding in his analysis of the event. Paludan's *A People's Contest: The Union and the Civil War, 1861-1865* is an outstanding study, but I consider *Victims* a better read.

James M. McPherson's **Battle Cry of Freedom: The Civil War Era** is the best extended summary of the war and its context. I wrote in a review for the *Atlanta Constitution*, "McPherson has not surpassed the achievements of Nevins, Catton, or Foote in volume, detail, or prose style. But the conclusions and questions of his history seem more consequential in this historical moment."

Will Campbell and the Soul of the South by Thomas L. Connelly is an obscure book and not directly about the Civil War. But it is the only work of non-fiction I ever willingly remained awake until 3:30 A.M. to finish. And like lots of things Southern which are not directly about the Civil War, they are really about nothing else.

Grant: A Biography by William S. McFeely is a masterpiece. It is about Grant, but more about the human condition.

EMORY M. THOMAS is Regents Professor of History at the University of Georgia at Athens. His many books on the Civil War include *The Confederacy as a Revolutionary Experience* and *The Confederate Nation 1861- 65.*

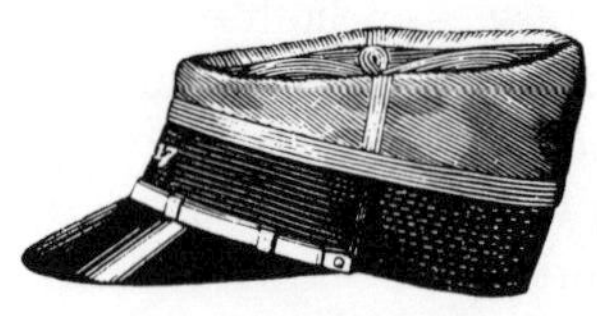

JOHN S.D. EISENHOWER ON MILITARY HISTORY

As the subject of military history is so broad, the only criterion I can use would be if I were limited to the posession of six books on military history (other than my own), what would they be? I would list them as follows:

Douglas Southall Freeman, **Lee's Lieutenants** (3 volumes)
Ulysses S. Grant, **Memoirs** (2 volumes)
Justin H. Smith, **The War With Mexico** (2 volumes)
Lucian K. Truscott, Jr., **Command Missions**
William Weber Johnson, **Heroic Mexico**. Has to do with the Mexican Revolution, 1911 to the present.

All of the above are masterpieces. And at the risk of being immodest, I might add that my own account of the Battle of the Bulge, *The Bitter Woods*, has held up very well through the years.

In that regard, I'm reminded of a story regarding Frank Lloyd Wright. When on the witness stand for some inquiry, he was asked to name the greatest architect in the world. He answered, "I am." When a friend chided him for immodesty, Wright replied, "What could I do? I was under oath."

JOHN S.D. EISENHOWER is a military historian whose books include *So Far From God: The U.S. War with Mexico, 1846-48.* He was a U.S. Army officer from 1944 to 1963 and served as a battalion officer during the Korean War.

JOHN KEEGAN ON MILITARY HISTORY

Thucydides, **The Peloponnesian War**. The first modern work of history, which is also an account of a major conflict by a participant.

Victor Hanson, **The Western Way of Warfare**. An American classical historian's revolutionary analysis of warfare in the Greek world, advancing the argument that the Greeks of the 5th century B.C. invented the idea of the "decisive battle."

John Guilmartin, **Gunpowder and Galleys**. An explanation of the part that warfare played in the life of the 16th century Mediterranean world, but also a brilliant exposition of the nature of naval warfare in general.

William H. McNeill, **The Pursuit of Power**. The nearest thing available to a complete history of warfare from the earliest times and a brilliantly intelligent book.

Michael Howard, **The Franco-Prussian War**. A model of how the history of a war should be written, by the world's leading military historian of the present day.

Chester Wilmot, **The Struggle for Europe**. An account of the origins and course of the Anglo-American liberation of Europe in the Second World War, which set the pattern for the writing of contemporary military history.

JOHN KEEGAN was a senior lecturer at the Royal Military Academy at Sandhurst before becoming defense editor of *The Daily Telegraph* in London. He is the author of *The Mask of Command*, *The Face of Battle*, and *A History of Warfare*.

PAUL WARNKE ON THE NUCLEAR AGE

The Making of the Atomic Bomb by Richard Rhodes. This is a rich and gripping account of the men and technology that gave rise to the atomic bomb and its eventual use in Hiroshima and Nagasaki.

Missile Madness by Herbert Scoville and Robert Osborn. Written on the eve of the first Strategic Arms Limitation Talks between the United States and the Soviet Union, this is a simple and comprehensible description of the nuclear arms race as it then stood. Scoville's informed comments and Osborn's arresting cartoons set forth the basics of the nuclear arms race and its dangers.

Stemming the Tide: Arms Control in the Johnson Years by Glenn T. Seaborg. Dr. Seaborg sets forth, in highly readable prose, an insider's account of the genesis and early conduct of the arms control process.

Nuclear Fallacy by Morton A. Halperin. In about 150 compelling pages, Dr. Halperin explodes the inflated notion that nuclear weapons convey exploitable military power. His book contributes to the growing recognition that, although the nuclear genie can't be put back in the bottle, it can be tamed and relegated to a minor role.

War and Peace in the Nuclear Age by John Newhouse. This is a companion book to the 13-part documentary television series produced for the PBS network. Brilliantly researched and written, it is an invaluable source of information about the people, the policies, and debates that characterized the five decades of nuclear confrontation between the Soviet Union and the United States.

Blundering into Disaster: Surviving the First Century of the Nuclear Age by Robert S. McNamara. Former Secretary of Defense Robert McNamara is the acknowledged father of strategic arms control. From his years of experience, McNamara shows how nuclear technology outpaced coherent policy development and brought us to the brink of nuclear calamity. He states his conclusion that "Nuclear weapons serve no military purpose whatsoever. They are totally useless — except to deter one's opponents from using them." Happily, with the end of the Cold War, many of his proposals have now been adopted.

PAUL C. WARNKE has long been a leading voice in national security and arms control policy circles. He served as general counsel of the Defense Department and as Assistant Secretary of Defense for International Security Affairs under President Johnson, and was Chief U.S. Arms Negotiator under President Carter.

CHAPTER 9
THE WORLD COMMUNITY

The booklists in this chapter introduce us to the farthest reaches of the world in ways that promise to expand our sometimes narrow personal horizons. By giving us a sense of our place in the overall scheme of things — the "big picture," as it has been called — they help us see that our world is only getting smaller, and nothing could be more fruitful than getting to know the neighbors.

PETER GZOWSKI ON CANADA

Sunshine Sketches of a Little Town by Stephen Leacock. It may come as a surprise to non-Canadians that well before Lucy Maude Montgomery gave the world *Anne of Green Gables* and long before Margaret Atwood or (barely) Robertson Davies were born, the author who reached our greatest international audience was a humorist. But Stephen Leacock, by day a gloomy political economist at

McGill University (and a staunch defender of the Empire), wrote more funny essays and gave more funny speeches than anyone north of Mark Twain. The *Sketches*, which ran originally as a series in the *Montreal Star*, are probably his most enduring, not very thinly disguised portraits of Orillia, Ontario, the small town where Leacock summered and wrote — and wrote and wrote. No knee-slappers, perhaps — and Garrison Keillor doesn't get them, he has said — but wry (and sometimes rye) snapshots of a gentler age.

Who Has Seen the Wind by W.O. Mitchell. The most evocative novel ever written about the Canadian — or North American, for that matter — prairie. Mitchell, who wrote this work when he was in his early 30s, has since authored dozens of radio plays, some works for the stage, and a number of other novels, but some critics have argued that he never did match his early masterpiece. Who cares?

The Hockey Sweater by Roch Carrier. Only a short story and only — ostensibly — for children, by a writer whose works also include essays, volumes of poems, and much more ambitious novels — *La Guerre, Yes Sir*, among them. But a wonderful, bittersweet portrait of a Quebec that was, and the absolute pervasion of both the church and Canada's national game into boyhood.

The Apprenticeship of Duddy Kravitz by Mordecai Richler. As urbane (there's a pun in there for Richler scholars) as Carrier is naif. The first full flowering of a writer Canadians themselves have trouble with (he's a bit too crotchety) but still laugh with. Like much of Richler, *Duddy* is Dickensian in its richness.

Anything by Margaret Laurence — though **The Stone Angel**, if there's only to be one — plus any of Robertson Davies's **Deptford Trilogy**, though, again, **Fifth Business**, if there's just one — and, just to have one book that no one else has heard of, a slim and near perfect novel from eastern Ontario called **The Lark in the Clear Air** by Dinnis Patrick Sears.

PETER GZOWSKI is the host of "Morningside," CBC's daily radio program. Previously, he was editor of *Maclean's* magazine. He is the author of *The Morningside Papers.*

MOLLY IVINS ON TEXAS

The Gay Place by William Brammer. A novel, still the best portrait of LBJ ever done.

Goodbye to a River by John Graves. A loving look at the landscape.

Lone Star by T.R. Fehrenbach. The best basic history.

In a Narrow Grave: Essays on Texas by Larry McMurtry. Wonderful feel of Texas past and passing.

The Great Frontier by Walter Prescott Webb. Explores all the important themes.

MOLLY IVINS is a columnist with the *Fort Worth Star-Telegram* and author of *Molly Ivins Can't Say That, Can She?*, and *Nothing But Good Times Ahead.*

HECTOR PEREZ-BRIGNOLI ON CENTRAL AMERICA

The Political Economy of Central America Since 1920 by Victor Bulmer-Thomas.

Central America: A Divided Nation by Ralph Lee Woodward.

The United States and the Caribbean in the Twentieth Century by Lester D. Langley.

Sons of the Shaking Earth by Eric R. Wolf.

Inevitable Revolutions: The United States in Central America by Walter LaFeber.

Spanish Central America: A Socioeconomic History, 1520-1920 by Murdo MacLeod.

Incidents of Travel in Central America: Chiapas and Yucatan by John L. Stephens (2 volumes).

HECTOR PEREZ-BRIGNOLI is a professor of history at the National University of Costa Rica. He is the author of *A Brief History of Central America* and, with Carolyn Hall, *An Historical Atlas of Central America.*

E. BRADFORD BURNS ON CENTRAL AMERICA

The Costa Rican historian Hector Perez-Brignoli provides a brilliant introduction to major historical themes in his interpretive **A Brief History of Central America**.

John A. Booth and Thomas W. Walker summarize and discuss the political and economic crises that have shaken the region during the last quarter of the 20th century in their brief and interpretive **Understanding Central America**.

Hunger stalks Central America. Malnutrition takes a fearful toll. Tom Barry points out in **Roots of Rebellion: Land and Hunger in Central America** the reasons why Central America no longer feeds itself, and the consequences.

Tom Barry and Rachel Garst have written a book illuminating this basic topic of the relationship of society to food production, **Feeding the Crisis: U.S. Food Aid and Farm Policy in Central America**.

A very human side to the drama of Central America appears in the autobiographical account of a Honduran peasant woman, **Don't Be Afraid, Gringo: A Honduran Woman Speaks from the Heart: The Story of Elvia Alvarado**, translated and edited by Medea Benjamin.

Literature provides a splendid insight into Central American society. The 1917 novel by Carlos Gagini (1865-1925), **Redemptions: A Costa Rican Novel**, discusses questions of emerging nationalism and concerns of economic development.

The Guatemalan novelist Miguel Angel Asturias (1899-1974) won the Nobel Prize for literature in 1967. His masterpiece, **The President**, depicts the daily reality of dictatorship and repression in early 20th century Guatemala.

A more recent account of Central American political reality is the powerful Salvadorean novel **One Day of Life** by Manlio Argueta. It depicts a typical peasant family caught up in the daily violence of civil war.

Testimony: Death of a Guatemalan Village by Victor Montejo provides an eyewitness account by a primary school teacher of an army attack on a Guatemalan village and its tragic aftermath. Taken together, Asturias, Argueta, and Montejo document the tragedy of violence that characterizes and shapes 20th century Central America.

The lyric voice of Central America arises from the many poets who populated and populate the isthmus. Foremost among them ranks the great Nicaraguan poet, Ruben Dario (1867-1916), still considered to be one of the finest poets ever to have written in the Spanish language. Consider Lysander Kemp's translation of **Selected Poems of Ruben Dario**.

Nicaragua is also the home of one of the most outstanding Latin America contemporary poets, Ernesto Cardenal. Some of his socially conscious poetry appears in **Apocalypse and Other Poems**.

E. BRADFORD BURNS has taught Latin American history at the University of California at Los Angeles since 1969. He is an essayist and the author of more than a dozen books on the history of the region, including a widely used textbook, *Latin America: A Concise Interpretive History*. He also wrote *Patriarch and Folk: The Emergence of Nicaragua*.

JORGE CASTANEDA ON MEXICO

Alan Riding, **Distant Neighbors**
Dick Reavis, **Conversations with Moctezuma**
Robert Pastor and Jorge Castañeda, **Limits to Friendship: The U.S. and Mexico**

JORGE CASTAÑEDA is a professor of international relations at the National Autonomous University of Mexico. He is author of *The Latin American Left and the Fall of Communism* and, with Robert Pastor, *Limits to Friendship: The United States and Mexico.*

CARMELO MESA-LAGO ON CUBA

Cuba: From Columbus to Castro by Jaime Suchlicki, 3rd edition. A summary of Cuba's history from the discovery of the island to the socialist revolution; simple and easy to read; fair as a first introduction.

Fidel: A Critical Portrait by Tad Szulc. A journalist's biography of Castro.

Cuban Communism, edited by Irving Louis Horowitz, 7th edition. A collection of essays on Cuban history, economy, society, politics, and armed forces.

Socialist Cuba: Past Interpretation and Future Challenges, edited by Sergio Roca. Another collection of essays (shorter but better integrated and more recent than the previous one) on politics, economy, and society.

Cuba After Thirty Years: Rectification and the

Revolution, edited by Richard Gillespie. Another collection focusing on Cuba at the end of the 1980s.

Cuba: Order and Revolution by Jorge Dominguez. An excellent treatise on Cuban politics from 1902 to the late 1970s.

To Make a World Safe for Revolution by Jorge Dominguez. Best book on Cuba's foreign policy.

The Economics of Cuban Sugar by Jorge Perez-Lopez. Profound analysis of Cuba's most important industry and source for exports.

Castro, the Blacks and Africa by Carlos Moore. Detailed and controversial study of race relations on the island and of Cuba's involvement in Africa.

Cuban Studies, volumes 16-20, edited by Carmelo Mesa-Lago. A multi-disciplinary yearbook entirely devoted to the study of Cuba; includes articles, bibliography, debates, and book reviews.

CARMELO MESA-LAGO is a professor of economics and Latin American affairs at the University of Pittsburgh. Born in Cuba, Mesa-Lago came to the United States in the early 1960s. He is the author of *Cuba in the 1970s* and *The Economy of Socialist Cuba*.

ROBERT FREEMAN SMITH ON CUBA

Cuba: The Pursuit of Freedom by Hugh Thomas. An encyclopedic history that is also balanced and well written. A good introduction to any aspect of Cuban history.

Cuba: From Columbus to Castro by Jaime Suchlicki. Much shorter than the Thomas volume, but an excellent presentation of the basics of Cuban history.

Cuba by Erna Ferguson. A popularly written account of life in mid-20th century Cuba blended with history. This is in the best tradition of informative "travel" literature.

Cuban Counterpoint: Tobacco and Sugar by Fernando Ortiz. This is a classic, almost poetic, interpretation of the development of Cuban society. This development, according to Ortiz, has been a counterpoint produced by the dramatic dialogue between "Don Tobacco and Doña Sugar."

Cuba: Its People, Its Society, Its Culture by Wyatt MacGaffey and Clifford R. Barnett. A comprehensive, readable volume that covers almost every element of Cuban society. There are chapters on ethnic influences, religion, education, as well as ones covering politics, economics, and foreign relations.

The America of José Martí: Selected Writings, edited by Federico de Onis. The best way to understand one of the monumental figures in Cuban history is to read what he wrote on a variety of subjects. In this excellent compendium one can sample Martí's thoughts on such topics as the society and culture of the United States, the culture of Latin

America, the nature of Cuban society, and the destiny of Cuba. Martí has been called one of the "finest interpreters" of "the other America."

The Role of the Military in the Making of the Cuban Republic by M. Hernandez. A scholarly analysis of a key factor in modern Cuban history.

The Cuban Policy of the United States: A Brief History by Lester D. Langley. A convenient coverage of the history of relations between the United States and the island. This book is a good starting point for more in-depth study.

The Unsuspected Revolution: The Birth and Decline of Castroism by Mario Llerena. A fascinating insider's account of the development of Castroism. The author, a former associate of Castro's, provides a careful analysis of what happened to change the nature of the "Revolution."

The Cuban Revolution by Hugh Thomas. Perhaps the best in-depth analysis of all aspects of the Castro Revolution from 1952 to 1962. Gives due significance to the historical roots. It has been labeled "monumental," "encyclopedic," as well as a work that is "immensely readable."

Response to Revolution: The U.S. and the Cuban Revolution, 1959-1961 by Richard E. Welch, Jr. The most balanced and well researched analysis of the U.S. response (both government and private) to the Cuban Revolution. The author shows that U.S. policymakers were basically in tune with American society, and places the events within the broader, international context.

Guerrilla Prince: The Untold Story of Fidel Castro by Georgie Anne Geyer. One of the best insights into the character of Castro and the nature of Castroism by a very honest journalist. Based on over 500 interviews, this book examines in detail Castro's formative years, and convincingly argues that he is not a communist but an absolute ruler for whom personal power is the only doctrine.

Reflections on the Cuban Missile Crisis by Raymond L. Garthoff. One of the best researched and complete analyses of the most dangerous crisis of the Cold War. This work gains added validity by its use of recent revelations from both Cuban and Soviet sources.

Against All Hope: The Prison Memoirs of Armando Valladares by Armando Valladares. The author spent 22 years in a Cuban prison for disagreeing with Fidel Castro. The sheer horror of Castro's prisons is fully revealed and we see the true face of the Castro Revolution. Apologists for Castro failed to discredit Valladares, and he played an important role in persuading the United Nations organization to investigate human rights violations in Cuba.

ROBERT FREEMAN SMITH is Distinguished University Professor at the University of Toledo. His books include *Background to Revolution: The Devlopment of Modern Cuba*; *What Happened in Cuba? A Documentary History of U.S.-Cuban Relations*; and *The United States and the Caribbean World, 1945-1991.*

TAD SZULC ON CUBA

Castro and the United States by Philip Bonsal.
Castroism: Theory and Practice by Theodore Draper.

TAD SZULC is a journalist and author. For nearly 20 years, he was a foreign correspondent for *The New York Times*, for which he covered the Bay of Pigs invasion. His books include *Fidel: A Critical Portrait; Then and Now*; and *The Secret Alliance.*

BASIL DAVIDSON ON AFRICA

Five books which are invaluable to the understanding of Africa:

Roland Oliver, **The African Experience**. For an introduction to Africa's long and extraordinary history.
Godfrey Lienhardt, **Divinity and Experience**. For the ideas and belief systems of African peoples, in this case the Dinka.
Max Gluckman, **The Ideas in Barotse Jurisprudence**. For the structures and principles of African legal systems, in this case the Barotse.
Ibn Khaldun, **The Muqaddimah**, first published circa 1395, translated by Franz Rosenthal. A great medieval history of, chiefly, the North Africans.
Chinua Achebe, **Anthills of the Savannah**. For a moving picture of the crisis-ridden plight of the Africa which has

come out of the years of colonial dispossession by Europe; a fine novel.

My own *vade mecum* in writing history, and because on any count it is a great read as well as a vivid telling of the origins of modern nationalism: **The Biography of Giuseppe Garibaldi** by George Macaulay Trevelyan in three volumes.

BASIL DAVIDSON is the author of over two dozen books on Africa, including *The Lost Cities of Africa*; *The African Genius: An Introduction to African Cultural and Social History*; *Black Star: A View of the Life and Times of Kwame Nkrumah*; and *Modern Africa.*

PATRICK O'MEARA AND C.R.D. HALISI ON SOUTH AFRICA

African Patriots: The Story of the African National Congress of South Africa by Mary Benson. Benson's study is one of the most outstanding examinations of the origin and development of the African National Congress.

Black Power in South Africa: The Evolution of an Ideology by Gail M. Gerhart. Gerhart's book is a definitive statement on the history, ideology, and importance of different African nationalist movements in South Africa.

Burger's Daughter by Nadine Gordimer. A Nobel Prize winner for literature, Gordimer deals with the involvement of a white middle class woman in the African liberation struggle.

Let My People Go: An Autobiography by Albert Luthuli. This book by Nobel Peace Prize winner Luthuli deals with his life as a central figure in the African National Congress and about the constraints of white official policy.

The Struggle is My Life by Nelson Mandela, revised edition.The speeches and other writings by Nelson Mandela present a vivid picture of the African liberation struggle and provide insights into the personality of this important leader.

Down Second Avenue by Ezikiel Mphaphele, 2nd edition. This novel presents a poignant and moving description of the poverty and struggles of Africans in the urban townships of South Africa.

Native Life in South Africa Before and Since the European War and Boer Rebellion by Sol Plaatje.

Time Longer than Rope: A History of the Black Man's Struggle for Freedom in South Africa by Edward Roux, 2nd edition. A book which first appeared nearly 50 years ago, this is an important study of black political resistance.

Class and Colour in South Africa, 1850-1950 by H.J. Simons and R.E. Simons. A major history of the nationalist and labor opposition to both segregation and apartheid.

The Politics of Race, Class and Nationalism in 20th Century South Africa by Shula Marks and Stanley Trapido. Includes bibliographic references. A collection of essays on the interconnectedness of race, class, and nationalism in South Africa, with chapters on Africans, Coloureds, and Indian communities.

PATRICK O'MEARA is a professor of political science and director of the African Studies Program at Indiana University. His books include *Rhodesia: Racial Conflict or Coexistence?*; *International Politics in Southern Africa*, written with Gwendolen Carter; and *African Independence: The First Twenty-Five Years.*

C.R.D. HALISI is an assistant professor of political science at Indiana University.

VALENTIN MUDIMBE ON AFRICA

Poetry:

Leopold Sedar Senghor, **Prose and Poetry.** This book is a magnificent marriage of an African sensibility and a French Cartesian legacy. It witnesses to the rich complexity, not only of being African, but of looking at things, facts, beings, and history as constituting glorious and infinite bodies.

Novels and autobiography:

Chinua Achebe, **Things Fall Apart**. A careful and imaginative report of the clash between two worlds: the conquering West and Africa. It masterfully depicts the naivetes of colonization and resilience of the old local tradition.

Ken Bugul, **The Abandoned Baobab**: **The Autobiography of a Senegalese Woman**. The sad journey of an African woman through European modernity and her own consciousness and feelings.

Cheik Hamidou Kane, **Ambiguous Adventure**. How to

reconcile an African Islamic tradition and a Cartesian understanding of the world. The hero of the novel, Samba Diallo, tries to make it and dies miserably, proving at the same time that the project is both thinkable and possible.

Wole Soyinka, **The Interpreters**. An imaginative novel about what it is like to live out an intercultural experience by the Nigerian Nobel Prize winner.

Essays:

Thomas O. Beidelman, **Moral Imagination in Kaguru Modes of Thought**. A masterful ethnographic study of an East African community and its process of producing an ethic in accord with its tradition.

Henry L. Gates, **The Signifying Monkey**. The best attempt to link the traditions of West Africa with African-American cultures from a literary viewpoint.

Luc de Heusch, **The Drunken King**. A structuralist analysis of founding myths of the state in Central and Southern Africa.

Paulin J. Hountondji, **African Philosophy: Myth and Reality**. What is African philosophy? How to understand the concept and relate the practice of "Weltanschaungen" to a demanding practice of philosophy.

Albert Memmi, **The Colonizer and the Colonized**. An acute sociological analysis of the master-slave relationship during the colonial era.

Jan Vansina, **Paths in the Rainforests: Toward a History of Political Tradition in Equatorial Africa**. A masterful synthesis of 3000 years of history in equatorial Africa.

Susan Vogel, editor, **Africa Explores: 20th Century African Art**. A critical synthesis of the 20th century trends in art. The book is, in fact, a catalog of an exhibit and is well illustrated.

VALENTIN Y. MUDIMBE is a professor of Romance Studies, comparative literature, and cultural anthropology at Duke University. His books include *The Invention of Africa*, *Parables and Fables*, and *The Idea of Africa*.

JEFFREY ARCHER ON ENGLAND

I was influenced greatly by Dickens's **Tale of Two Cities** at one end and Lord Blake's **Disraeli** at the other end.

JEFFREY ARCHER is a novelist and a former British Member of Parliament. His novels include *Not a Penny More, Not a Penny Less*; *Kane and Abel*; *First Among Equals*; and *Honor Among Thieves*.

England is the paradise of individuality, eccentricity,
heresy, anomalies, hobbies, and humors.
— George Santayana

LARRY AND ROBERTA GARNER ON ITALY

We have focused on history, society, and politics as well as literature that addresses social and cultural topics. Ginsborg's book is our "desert island choice" — an up-to-date, budget conscious, and thoroughly professional account of contemporary Italy.

Classics:

The Divine Comedy by Dante. A poet's vision of Hell, Purgatory, and Heaven; a work that marks the end of the Middle Ages and the beginning of Italian literature.

The Prince by Machiavelli. A book of no-holds-barred advice on how to exercise power that has fascinated readers since the Renaissance.

History and civilization, the Renaissance:

The Civilization of the Renaissance in Italy by Jacob Burckhardt. A classic portrait of the Renaissance as the first modern way of life—its origins, values and beliefs.

The Italian Renaissance by J.H. Plumb. A short, readable introduction with chapters on city life and women as well as art and culture.

The Rise and Fall of the House of Medici by Christopher Hibbert. A well-written account of life in Florence that traces the emergence of the Renaissance, its cultural high point, and the decline that set in during the 16th and 17th centuries.

History and civilization, modern Italy:

Italy: A Modern History by Denis Mack-Smith. The best general account of Italian history in the 19th century and the first two-thirds of the 20th century, covering the formation of the Italian state, Mussolini and fascism, and the establishment of the Italian republic at the end of World War II.

Contemporary Italy, social, economic, and political issues:

A History of Contemporary Italy: Society and Politics, 1943-1988 by Paul Ginsborg. Excellent and up-to-date. For the reader who is looking for the best single book on contemporary Italian society and politics.

A Political History of Italy: The Post-War Years by Norman Kogan. Charts the course of Italian politics — its stable character, despite the appearance of many changes in government.

Contemporary Italy: Politics, Economy, Society by Donald Sassoon. An excellent overview of the post-World War II period for the reader with an interest in the social sciences.

20th century literature:

Plays by Luigi Pirandello. Probably the best collection is **Naked Masks**, edited by Eric Bentley. Italy's greatest playwright, known for his ironic reflections on the nature of reality, "truth," and madness.

Two Women by Alberto Moravia. A Roman mother and daughter struggle to survive during World War II.

The Conformist by Alberto Moravia. Explores the psycho-sexual roots of collaboration with fascism.

Bread and Wine by Ignazio Silone. One man's commitment to resist fascism.

The Leopard by Giuseppe Tomasi Di Lampedusa. A beautiful novel about the reluctant integration of Sicily into modern Italy and the fortunes of the Sicilian aristocracy.

The distinct history, culture, and economic conditions of the South of Italy pose ongoing problems for Italian integration, including economic underdevelopment and the power of the Mafia. The following three books provide some insights into the origins of these issues.

Patronage, Power, and Poverty in Southern Italy by Judith Chubb. Insight into the connections between politicians and Mafia in contemporary Italy.

Christ Stopped at Eboli by Carlo Levi. A poetic evocation of Southern customs and beliefs, written by an artist sent to a small Southern town by the fascists — a classic.

The Leopard by Di Lampedusa. See above.

LARRY GARNER teaches political science at DePaul University. With Roberta Garner he has published articles on Italy in *Current History* and *Science and Society*.

ROBERTA GARNER is a professor of sociology at DePaul University. She has published articles on Jacob Burckhardt and the Renaissance in *Sociological Theory* and on Italian schooling in *Urban Education*.

STANLEY HOFFMANN ON FRANCE

On France:

The Old Regime and the French Revolution by Alexis de Tocqueville. Still the best political sociology of that infernal couple: the French state and French society.

France 1848-1945 by Theodore Zeldin. A superb, scholarly "history" which is really a series of essays on French thought, life, and mores.

Village in the Vaucluse by Laurence Wylie. The best "village study" by a subtle and empathetic student of French civilization.

War Memoirs by Charles de Gaulle (5 volumes). A great epic work, indispensable for an understanding of the French crisis of decline and renewal in this century.

Sentimental Education by Gustave Flaubert. The best French historical novel: a disgruntled view of French society around 1848.

Books important to me:

The Social Contract by Jean-Jacques Rousseau. The most profound democratic utopia (also essential for understanding the French Revolution and French Republicanism).

Les Thibault by Roger Martin du Gard. A huge novel that is to France in the early 20th century what Tolstoi's *War and Peace* is to early 19th century Russia.

The Plague by Albert Camus. Austere allegory of totalitarianism (and of death).

Antigone by Jean Anouilh. A modern version of the Greek tragedy that shows ethical and civic duties in mortal conflict.
Kant, his ethical philosophy.

STANLEY HOFFMANN is a professor of political science and chairman of the Center for European Studies at Harvard University. His books include *In Search of France* and *Decline or Renewal: France Since the 1930s.*

NICHOLAS RIASANOVSKY ON EASTERN EUROPE

Trying to name the most valuable 10 books for as large and vaguely defined an area as "Eastern Europe" is an almost hopeless task, but the following books cover most of the geographic area and provide extensive bibliographies for further reading.

Barbara Jelavich, **History of the Balkans** (2 volumes). Gives the reader a background to the national passions that underlie the present-day Yugoslav conflict.
Norman Davies, **God's Playground: A History of Poland** (2 volumes). Traces the history of Poland from its beginnings. Readable and comprehensive.
Ezra Mendelsohn, **The Jews of East Central Europe Between the Two World Wars**. Before 1939, the largest Jewish community in the world lived in East Central Europe. Their history is given in this volume, which covers the entire region.
A.J.P. Taylor, **The Habsburg Monarchy, 1809-1918**.

Still the best general introduction to the Habsburg Empire's final century of existence. Short and concise.

R.J.W. Evans, **The Making of the Habsburg Monarchy 1550-1700: An Interpretation**. Provides a stimulating thesis on the political and intellectual bases of the Habsburg monarchy while giving the reader an historical account of these formative years, including the period of the Thirty Years' War.

Robert K. Massie, **Peter the Great: His Life and World**. Popular, very readable, and full of details about the life and times of Russia's first "European" ruler.

Isabel de Madariaga, **Russia in the Age of Catherine the Great**. A thorough account of the intellectual, political, and social events of Catherine's reign.

Robert Conquest, **The Great Terror: A Reassessment**. Reexamines the period of Stalin's reign of terror, using newly available archival materials. Invaluable for understanding the Soviet state.

Richard Stites, **Revolutionary Dreams: Utopian Vision and Experimental Life in the Russian Revolution**. The utopian dreams and visions which were present at the beginnings of the Russian revolutionary experience. Important in documenting some of the intellectual possibilities envisioned immediately before and after the Bolshevik victory.

Richard Pipes, **The Russian Revolution**. Extremely thorough, extremely critical of Lenin and the Bolsheviks, but very solidly based on secondary and primary sources.

NICHOLAS RIASANOVSKY is a professor of history at the University of California at Berkeley. His books include *Russia and the West in the Teaching of the Slavophiles*; *A History of Russia*; and *A Parting of Ways: Government and the Educated Public in Russia, 1801-1855.*

EUGEN WEBER ON FRANCE

Montaigne, **Essays**. A distillation of human and humane wisdom: curious, tolerant, skeptical, and accessible.

Stendahl, **The Red and the Black**. An impossible hero sabotages his irresistible ascension. The epitome of French romanticism.

Balzac, **The Human Comedy**. Just what the collective title claims: the theatre of life at all social levels between the 1820s and the 1840s. If you can't swallow it entire, skim around to see which novel catches your fancy. **Father Goriot**, **Lost Illusions**, and **The Peasants** are among the most striking.

Flaubert, **The Sentimental Education**. The high hopes and illusions of a group of young men of the 1840s end in disillusion, but leave no taste of ashes in the mouth. A universally valid picture of growing up on a private income, and even without one, but also a marvelous account of the revolutions of 1848: one more turning point where history failed to turn.

Marc Bloch, **Strange Defeat**. A great historian and a good soldier muses on France's crumbling before German forces in the summer of 1940 and tries to trace the origins of the unexpected humiliation.

And two critical works still untranslated into English:

Jules Renard's **Journal** from 1887 to his death (aged 46) in 1910: just as nasty, clever and, informed as the Goncourts' *Journal*, but less provincial and more pithy.

Pierre Drieu La Rochelle's **Reveuse Bourgeoisie**, for middle-class life French-style before the Second World War. Crabs in a basket.

To your request to list books that have had an impact on me, I am tempted to answer the **Bible**, **The Oxford Book of English Verse**, and **Winnie the Pooh**. More to your point, however, the books that proved most important to me professionally were Lucien Febvre's **La Terre et L'Evolution Humaine**, Marc Bloch's **Feudal Society**, and Fernand Braudel's **Mediterranean**. Their content mattered far less than their style: the way they approached documentary material, the way they handled language. In each case, unintimidated by traditional rules and limits, they reached out to make both language and substance more vivid. Charles Peguy had done as much — another soldier-intellectual who jostled accepted categories, orthodoxies, and intellectual securities to show that safe values are the least reliable investments.

EUGEN WEBER is the Joan Palevsky Professor of Modern European History at the University of California at Los Angeles. His works include *Action Française, Peasants into Frenchmen*; *France Fin-de-Siecle*; and *France: The 1930s.*

Ideas, as distinguished from events,
are never unprecedented.
— Hannah Arendt

CARL SCHORSKE ON GERMANY

Goethe, **Faust**
Thomas Mann, **Stories of Three Decades**
Robert Musil, **The Man Without Qualities**
Jacob Burckhardt, **The Civilization of the Renaissance in Italy**
Karl Marx, **The German Ideology** and **Capital** (Volume 1)
Hannah Arendt, **Origins of Totalitarianism**

The first three works above explore the trials, successes, and crimes of modern European man in his German incarnation as conceived by literary artists. The second three works, by social analysts of German culture, give us original perspectives with which to make some historical meaning out of the human experience refracted by the writers.

CARL SCHORSKE is Professor Emeritus of History at Princeton University.His books include *The Problem of Germany; German Social Democracy, 1905-1917*; and *Fin de Siecle Vienna; Politics and Culture.*

MARSHALL I. GOLDMAN ON THE SOVIET UNION

Karl Marx and Friedrich Engels, **The Communist Manifesto**
Milovan Djilas, **The New Class**
Hedrick Smith, **The Russians** and **The New Russians**
Richard Pipes, **The Russian Revolution**
Adam Ulam, **The Bolsheviks**
Edmund Wilson, **To the Finland Station**
Mikhail Gorbachev, **Perestroika**

MARSHALL I. GOLDMAN is the associate director of the Russian Research Center at Harvard University. His many works on Soviet economic issues include *The Soviet Economy: Myth and Reality* and *U.S.S.R. in Crisis: The Failure of an Economic System.*

The workers have nothing to lose in this but
their chains. They have a world to gain.
Workers of the world, unite!
— Karl Marx and Friedrich Engels,
The Communist Manifesto

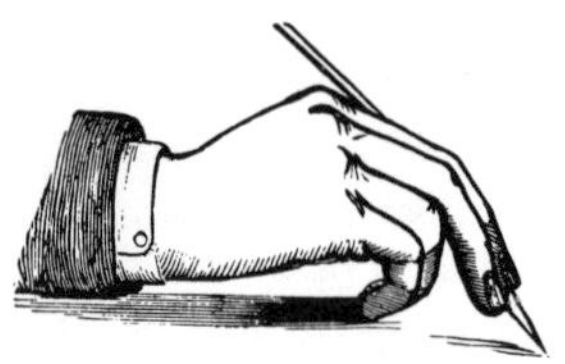

AFAF LUTFI AL-SAYYID MARSOT ON THE MIDDLE EAST

A History of the Arab Peoples by Albert Hourani. Covers the Arab world from the advent of Islam to the present. Easy to read and understand, it is the best book on the subject yet.

A History of the Middle East by Peter Mansfield. A readable book by a former British correspondent in the Middle East.

The Venture of Islam by Marshal Hodgson (3 volumes). A brilliant work but difficult to read because of new terminology. Not for the fainthearted.

Politics and Change in the Middle East by Roy R. Andersen et al. Covers the 20th century ably and succinctly.

The Gun and the Olive Branch by David Hirst. One of the few books giving both sides of the Arab-Israeli conflict and its origins in a neutral fashion, written by a former British correspondent.

A Decade of Decisions by William Quandt. A member of the National Security Council writes on conflicts in the Middle East and U.S. policy towards the region.

Rich and Poor States in the Middle East by Malcolm Kerr and El Sayed Yassin. Some excellent articles on the effects of petro-dollars on the region in social and economic terms. Both the good side and the negative aspects of wealth and poverty.

Modern Islamic Political Thought by Hamid Enayat. One of the few books which compares the teachings of sunni Islam with that of shii Islam with regards to society and politics. Ranges from thinkers of the classical age to the present.

Muhammad by Martin Lings. The latest biography of the Prophet Muhammad, using 8th and 9th century Arabic sources, written by a man who is a mystic and representing the best of the biographies to date. A must for those wishing to understand Islam.

Autumn of Fury by M.H. Heikal. A deliciously malicious view of Sadat by an Egyptian journalist who was Nasser's right hand man, but a view shared by a large number of Egyptians.

Women In the Muslim World, edited by Lois Beck and Nikki Keddie. Thirty-three articles on women in various societies; nomadic, settled, urban, and rural. Still one of the best on the subject.

Cheapest Nights by Yudif Idris. A collection of short stories by the foremost short story writer in the Arab world. Sensitive and evocative writing.

Miramar by Naguib Mahfouz. A touching and beautiful

novel by Egypt's Nobel Prize winner. His most readable and comprehensible novel to Western audiences.

Islam by Fazlur Rahman, 2nd edition. The religion of the majority of the Middle East explained in simple terms without oversimplification.

AFAF LUTFI AL-SAYYID MARSOT teaches Middle East history at the University of California at Los Angeles, specializing in the role of women in the Muslim world. She is the author of *A Short History of Modern Egypt* and editor of *Society and the Sexes in Medieval Islam.*

EDWARD PECK ON IRAQ

Samir al Khalil, **Republic of Fear: the Politics of Modern Iraq**. Well documented but passionate criticism.

Efraim Karsh and Inari Rautsi, **Saddam Hussein: A Political Biography**

Helen Metz, editor, **Iraq: A Country Study**, 4th edition

Amatzia Baram, **Culture, History and Ideology in the Formation of Ba'athist Iraq, 1968-1989**

These four will suffice, I think, for anyone except serious scholars.

EDWARD PECK was a career foreign service officer whose posts included Economic/Commercial Counselor in Egypt, Chief of Mission in Iraq, and Chief of Mission in Mauritania. He retired from the State Department in 1989 and is currently a consultant.

MARVIN ZONIS ON THE MIDDLE EAST

Arabic Political Memoirs and Other Studies by Elie Kedourie.

A Peace to End All Peace by David Fromkin.

Islamic Liberalism: A Critique of Development Ideologies by Leonard Binder.

The Turban for the Crown by Said Amir Arjomand.

Debating Muslims: Cultural Dialogues in Post-Modernity and Tradition by Michael Fischer and Mehdi Abedi.

Self-Involvement in the Middle East Conflict by the Committee on Foreign Relations.

Women of Deh Koh: Stories from Iran by Erika Friedl.

The Outlaw State by Elaine Sciolino.

The Immortal Ataturk by Vamik D. Volkan and Norman Itzkowitz.

MARVIN ZONIS teaches Soviet and Middle Eastern politics at the University of Chicago. He is the author of several books on the region, including *Majestic Failure: The Fall of the Shah of Iran* and *The East European Opportunity.*

PERRY LINK ON CHINA

Edward Friedman, Paul Pickowicz, and Mark Selden, **Chinese Village, Marxist State: The Story of Wu Gong Village**. The best account of village life in Communist China.

Simon Leys, **Chinese Shadows**. A penetrating and acerbic account of China under Mao Zedong, by one of the best-informed Sinologists in the West.

Leo Ou-fan Lee, **Voices from the Iron House**. An analysis of the work of Lu Xun, China's most insightful writer in the early 20th century; to be read in conjunction with the next item.

Lu Xun, **Diary of a Madman and Other Stories**, translated by William Lyell.

Jonathan Spence, **The Search for Modern China**. The best general history of modern China. Stimulating, lucid, and solid.

Andrew Walder, **Communist Neo-Traditionalism: Work and Authority in Chinese Industry**. A sociological analysis of life in China's urban "work units."

EUGENE PERRY LINK, JR. is a professor of Chinese at Princeton University. His books include *Mandarin Ducks and Butterflies: Popular Fiction in Early Twentieth-Century Chinese Cities* and *Evening Chats in Beijing: Probing China's Predicament*, an account of the reflections and worries of intellectuals in China today.

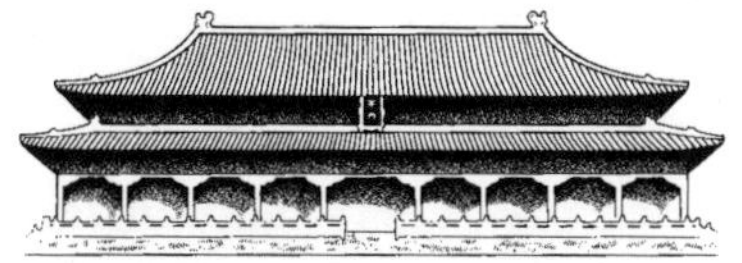

WINSTON LORD ON CHINA

Legacies by Bette Bao Lord. True stories of Chinese people that illuminate China under the Communists, 1949-1989, including China Spring 1989.

The Search for Modern China by Jonathan Spence. The best, most readable history of China from the 1600s.

Spring Moon by Bette Bao Lord. A beautiful novel of China that reveals much of China's history and culture in this 20th-century family story.

WINSTON LORD is Assistant Secretary of State for East Asian and Pacific Affairs. His former diplomatic and government posts have included serving on the National Security Council staff under President Nixon; director of the State Department policy planning staff under President Ford; and ambassador to China under President Reagan.

STEVEN MOSHER ON CHINA

Life and Death in Shanghai by Nien Cheng. The story of a patriotic and civilized woman who faces the full fury of the Red Guards during the Cultural Revolution, and who overcomes torture, humiliation, and unending psychological abuse with strength and dignity. A breathtaking testimony to the human spirit.

Wild Swans by Jung Chang. The true-life saga of the Chang family, and its struggle to survive in revolutionary China with its wars, violence, and continuing upheaval. Written by the daughter of a high-ranking Communist official, it is an important work of history.

Legacies by Bette Bao Lord. A series of snapshots of life in modern China, this book is beautifully written and hauntingly effective.

STEVEN W. MOSHER is the director of the Asian Studies Center at the Claremont Institute for the Study of Statemanship and Political Philosophy. He is the author of several books on China, including *A Mother's Ordeal* and *China Misperceived: American Illusions and Chinese Reality.*

DONALD RICHIE ON JAPAN

G.B. Sansom, **Japan: A Short Cultural History** and **The Western World and Japan**. Still the most balanced and judicious accounts of Japan and its culture. Subscribing to none of the *nihonjinron** theories, seasoned with a healthy skepticism of official sources, these two books continue to offer seasoned insight.

Thomas Raucat, **The Honourable Picnic**. A translation (from the French) of the finest single novel on the country. Written by an embassy official (under a pseudonym) it initially angered Japanese authorities, but now its affection and deep insight into the Japanese people have become apparent. Though a comic novel, and a very funny one, it offers a true understanding.

Kurt Singer, **Mirror, Sword and Jewel: A Study of Japanese Characteristics**. Though written in the 1940s from notes taken in the 1930s when Singer was in Japan, this connected series of *aperçus* concerning the country and the culture remains the most insightful. A classics scholar, Singer brought to this study a balanced knowledge which precisely describes and never theorizes.

Roland Barthes, **The Empire of Signs**. A translation of the original 1970 text, this work was composed after only several months in Japan, but the methodology imposed, and the insight displayed, make this a seminal book. Some of it is enmeshed in theory, but the theory is not that of the *nihonjinron* variety. Throughout, Japan is seen in Western terms which do not violate the integrity of the scene described.

Ivan Morris, **The Nobility of Failure**. In writing this study of "Tragic Heroes in the History of Japan," Morris approaches the Japanese character from a completely individual direction and is able to describe much that is otherwise unaccounted for in the ordinary appreciations of the country.

Karel van Wolferen, **The Enigma of Japanese Power**. The first description of political motivation in Japan which refuses to avail itself of the accepted half-truths of the *nihonjinron*. Perceived in Japan as an attack, the book is scarcely that, but it is a completely unsparing description. It strays into prescription as well, but its impact is considerable.

* *Nihonjinron* refers to that body of work (Reischauer et al.) which seeks to "explain" Japan through outmoded theory.

DONALD RICHIE is a cultural critic and writer who has lived in Japan for over 30 years. His books include *The Japanese Film: Art and Industry*; *Japanese Cinema: An Introduction*; and *A Lateral View: Essays on Culture and Style in Contemporary Japan*.

JUDITH SHAPIRO ON CONTEMPORARY CHINA

These are all first-person accounts of contemporary China:

Chinese Lives by Zhang Xinxin and Sang Ye. A kaleidoscope of ordinary Chinese voices — a Chinese "*Working.*"

Iron and Silk by Mark Salzman. A memoir by a Yale-in-China teacher who took the best China had to offer by immersing himself in its traditional arts. Shows the humor in life under totalitarianism.

A Higher Kind of Loyalty by Liu Binyan. A memoir by China's foremost dissident journalist.

The Early Arrival of Dreams by Rosemary Mahoney. A poignant look at the experience of teaching English in China, beautifully written and sensitively observed.

Life and Death in Shanghai by Nien Cheng. A searing memoir of abuse during the Cultural Revolution, by a sensitive, highly-educated victim.

Wild Swans by Jung Chang. A memoir of three generations of Chinese women illustrates the hope held out by the Communists and the despair they brought.

JUDITH SHAPIRO lectures and writes about China. She is a resident scholar at the Foreign Policy Research Institute in Philadelphia. Her books, which were written with Liang Heng, include *After the Nightmare* and *Cold Winds, Warm Winds.*

JONATHAN SPENCE ON CHINA

Confucius: The Analects, translated by D.C. Lau. The root text for China's main-line philosophical tradition.

The Complete Works of Chuang-Tzu, translated by Burton Watson. The brilliant "anti-text" to Confucius; basis of the Taoist tradition of free-fall thought.

The Story of the Stone by Cao Xueqin (also known as **The Dream of the Red Chamber**), translated by David Hawkes and John Minford. China's wondrous 18th-century novel of manners.

The True Story of AHQ by Lu Hsun, translated by Yang Hsien-Yi and Gladys Yang. The most piercing novella of the end of China's empire in 1911.

The August Sleepwalker by Bei Dao, translated by Bonnie McDougall. Beautiful, despairing poems of China under the Communist government.

JONATHAN SPENCE teaches modern Chinese history at Yale University, and is a MacArthur fellow. He is the author of more than a half-dozen books on China, including *The Question of Hu* and *The Search for Modern China.*

Index